NAVAL BATTLES OF
THE SECOND WORLD WAR

HMS Penelope *was an Arethusa class light cruiser which saw considerable action during the war, notably with the Malta-based Force K. While undergoing repairs there she was riddled with shrapnel from German bombs and gained the nickname 'HMS* Pepperpot'. *Eventually she was sunk by a U-boat attack off Anzio on 18 February 1944.* (NARA)

NAVAL BATTLES OF
THE SECOND WORLD WAR
The Atlantic and the Mediterranean

Leo Marriott

Pen & Sword
MARITIME

AN IMPRINT OF PEN & SWORD BOOKS LTD.
YORKSHIRE – PHILADELPHIA

First published in Great Britain in 2022 by
PEN & SWORD MARITIME
An imprint of
Pen & Sword Books Ltd
Yorkshire – Philadelphia

ISBN 978 1 39909 893 9

A CIP catalogue record for this book is
available from the British Library.

Typeset in Ehrhardt 11/13.5
by SJmagic DESIGN SERVICES, India.

Printed and bound in the UK by CPI Group (UK) Ltd.

Pen & Sword Books Ltd incorporates the imprints of Pen & Sword Archaeology, Atlas,
Aviation, Battleground, Discovery, Family History, History, Maritime, Military, Naval,
Politics, Social History, Transport, True Crime, Claymore Press, Frontline Books,
Praetorian Press, Seaforth Publishing and White Owl.

For a complete list of Pen & Sword titles please contact

PEN & SWORD BOOKS LTD
47 Church Street, Barnsley, South Yorkshire, S70 2AS, England
E-mail: enquiries@pen-and-sword.co.uk
Website: www.pen-and-sword.co.uk

or

PEN AND SWORD BOOKS
1950 Lawrence Rd, Havertown, PA 19083, USA
E-mail: Uspen-and-sword@casematepublishers.com
Website: www.penandswordbooks.com

Contents

Glossary and Abbreviations

The following list explains terms and abbreviations used in the text and also gives the key to abbreviations relating to ship types and nationality in the list contained in the appendix.

AA	Anti-Aircraft
a/c	Aircraft
ASV	Airborne surface search radar
AX	Auxiliary anti-aircraft vessel
BB	Battleship (US Navy designation)
CA	Heavy Cruiser (US Navy designation)
Captain (D)	Captain (Destroyers). RN Captain commanding a flotilla of destroyers
CB	Battlecruiser (US Navy designation)
C-in-C	Commander-in-Chief
CL	Light Cruiser (US Navy designation)
CM	Cruiser Minelayer
CS	Cruiser Squadron
CV	Aircraft Carrier (US Navy designation)
CVE	Escort carrier (US Navy designation)
CVS	Seaplane carrier (US Navy designation)
DD	Destroyer (US Navy designation)
DE	Escort Destroyer (RN) or Destroyer Escort (USN)
DF	Destroyer Flotilla
D/F	Direction Finding (from radio transmissions)
DSC	Distinguished Service Cross (British award)
DSO	Distinguished Service Order (British award)
Fra	France
Ger	Germany
grt	Gross Registered Tonnage
HMAS	His Majesty's Australian Ship

HMNZS	His Majesty's New Zealand Ship
HMS	His Majesty's Ship
H.No.M.S	His Norwegian Majesty's Ship
in	inch (unit of measurement)
It.N	Italian Navy
kt	knot (= 1 nautical mile per hour)
Magic	Code name applied to intelligence gathered by US codebreakers
MAS/MS	Italian designation for MTB type vessels
MGB	Motor Gun Boat
MTB	Motor Torpedo Boat
MV	Merchant Vessel
NAS	Naval Air Squadron
Neth	Netherlands
nm	nautical mile
Nor	Norway
PF	Frigates, corvettes and other escort vessels
Pol	Poland
Pzs	Panzerschiffe (armoured ship)
RAF	Royal Air Force
RAN	Royal Australian Navy
RN	Royal Navy
RNZN	Royal New Zealand Navy
TB	Torpedo Boat (small destroyer)
TF	Task Force
TT	Torpedo Tubes
Ultra	Intelligence information obtained by reading German messages originally encoded by an Enigma machine (cf. Magic)
US	United States
USN	United States Navy
USS	United States Ship
VC	Victoria Cross (British award)

Introduction

The Second World War was indeed a global conflict in which few nations were unaffected by the great events that took place from September 1939 to August 1945. As over two thirds of the earth's surface is covered by oceans and seas, it was inevitable that maritime power would play a major role in every theatre of the war. Even campaigns fought entirely on land, such as the Western Desert or the Russian Front, needed the support provided by convoys carrying fuel, ammunition, men and materiel, and the blocking of these supply lines would often have a disproportionate effect on the outcome of land battles being fought.

This book (and a companion volume) is intended as a basic guide to the main naval engagements in each theatre of operations covered. For more information there are numerous books that describe these actions in much greater detail and some of these are listed in the bibliography. To show how the various naval battles were connected to the events around them, the book is set out in sections, each dealing with a major ocean or sea, and within each section the engagements are linked in chronological order so that, together, they provide an overview of the history of the naval campaigns in that part of the world. This first volume covers the Atlantic and Arctic oceans, and the Mediterranean Sea, both areas in which the Royal Navy was the major force and the engagements described relate to its long struggle against the German and Italian navies. This includes, of course, the monumental Battle of the Atlantic, which lasted for five long years until May 1945 and was perhaps the most critical campaign of the whole war. In the Mediterranean the most significant actions resulted from the attempts of both sides to supply their armies in North Africa while trying to prevent the enemy from doing the same. The island of Malta became the key to this and convoys to supply it with food, fuel and ammunition became great set-piece battles.

The United States Navy was also involved in the Atlantic and, later, in the Mediterranean. However, it was in the vast expanses of the Pacific, where for almost four years a great maritime campaign ebbed and flowed, that its greatest battles were fought and these will be covered in a separate volume.

As Allied forces gradually took the offensive, the art of amphibious warfare was developed and refined on a grand scale. Unfortunately, most of the great amphibious enterprises were not naval battles in the conventional sense and so they have not been described in these volumes, although some of the engagements that are included occurred as a result of such operations.

Note: The map diagrams accompanying each battle description are intended to portray the basic outline of events and for the sake of clarity indicate only the general movements of the major units involved.

Part One
Atlantic Ocean and NW Europe

In 1939 the Royal Navy possessed an overwhelming numerical superiority over the German fleet and therefore massive encounters such as had been fought in the First World War were not going to happen. Instead, the Kriegsmarine opted for an all-out war against Britain's vital seaborne trade routes using both submarines and surface vessels. Even prior to the outbreak of war, it had deployed pocket battleships and other merchant raiders, and these swung into action as soon as hostilities were declared. They tied down significant naval resources as British and French ships combined to form search groups and these activities eventually led to the sinking of the *Graf Spee* in the Battle of the River Plate in December 1939. However, other warships, including the battlecruisers *Scharnhorst* and *Gneisenau*, the *Admiral Scheer*, and the heavy cruiser *Admiral Hipper*, all roamed the North Atlantic at various times up to late 1941 and achieved some successes in disrupting convoys and sinking merchant ships. It was to mount such an operation that the *Bismarck* and *Prinz Eugen* sailed from Germany in May 1941, leading to one of the most dramatic sea chases of all time, which culminated in the sinking of the German battleship. Thereafter, the remaining capital ships were concentrated in home and Norwegian waters, from where they could threaten the important Arctic convoys which, from 1941 onwards, carried supplies from Britain and the United States to their new Russian ally.

Norway had already been invaded and occupied by German forces in April 1940 in order to secure access to vital Scandinavian ore supplies, and it was also an important strategic base for warships and U-boats to break out into the Atlantic, as well as dominating the route to Russia. The German occupation of Norway did not go unchallenged and it saw some important naval actions. By July 1940, France had capitulated and their Atlantic ports now became available to the rapidly expanding German U-boat arm. From this point on the most important battle of the war was fought in the grey wastes of the Atlantic as the U-boats roamed far and wide, taking a massive toll of Allied shipping and coming very near to forcing Britain into submission. The eventual outcome of the Battle of the Atlantic depended as much on scientific innovation and industrial resources as it did on tactics and individual heroism.

From 1942 onwards, the focus of surface operations shifted to Norway and the protection of the Arctic convoys. The sinking of the *Scharnhorst* on Boxing Day

1943 was an important step forward and left only the *Tirpitz* as a major threat in this theatre (she was finally sunk by RAF bombers in November 1944). Her demise allowed the Royal Navy to redeploy major assets including battleships and aircraft carriers to the Eastern and Pacific fleets, where they could play an important role in the closing stages of the war against Japan.

Perhaps the greatest maritime enterprise ever attempted was Operation Overlord, the Allied invasion of northern France in June 1944. This required enormous naval resources, both to convey and protect the landing force, and to provide the necessary support once the troops were ashore. Strictly speaking, this was not a naval battle as enemy seaborne resistance was minimal, but it should not be forgotten that Overlord could never have been mounted had the Battle of the Atlantic not been won and had the German surface navy not been reduced to ineffectiveness by previous Allied air and naval actions.

Battle of the River Plate

Date:	13 December 1939
Location:	Estuary of the River Plate, between Argentina and Uruguay

Allied Forces

Commander:	Commodore Henry Harwood Harwood RN
Ships:	Heavy cruiser: HMS *Exeter*. Light cruisers: HMS *Ajax*, HMNZS *Achilles*

Axis Forces

Commander:	Kapitän zur See Hans Wilhelm Langsdorff
Ships:	Panzerschiffe: *Admiral Graf Spee*

BACKGROUND: The pocket battleship *Admiral Graf Spee* had sailed from Germany on 21 August 1939, before hostilities had begun, and headed for the open spaces of the South Atlantic, where she remained undetected until claiming her first victim on 30 September. In reaction to this the Admiralty organised hunting groups, comprising no less than four aircraft carriers, three battlecruisers and thirteen cruisers to reinforce the existing patrols in the South Atlantic and Indian oceans. Even if the *Graf Spee* had not sunk a single ship, this diversion of effort to track her down was a major success for the Germans. As it was, the *Graf Spee* claimed several further victims in the South Atlantic and Indian oceans. Later she headed towards the Plate estuary and on the morning of 13 December 1939 was some 300 miles east of Montevideo, Uruguay. In the meantime, Allied patrols had been searching fruitlessly for the elusive pocket battleship but one of Langsdorff's victims, the 10,086-ton *Doric Star*, got off a distress message before being sunk. Based on this report, Commodore Harwood, commander of the RN South American Division, made an inspired calculation of the *Graf Spee*'s likely actions, forecasting that she would be off the Plate estuary by 13 December, and instructed his scattered force of three cruisers to concentrate accordingly.

THE ACTION: As dawn broke on the 13th, Harwood's ships were in line ahead, steering north-east, when smoke was sighted at 0614 on a bearing of 324°. In accordance with his pre-planned tactics of trying to split the enemy's main armament, he ordered the 8in cruiser HMS *Exeter* to close and identify the unknown vessel while the two light cruisers continued on their original course. *Exeter* soon signalled that she had a pocket battleship in sight and two minutes later, the *Graf Spee* opened fire on her. For a while, Langsdorff continued to head south-east and chose to split his main armament, using one triple turret against *Exeter* and the other against *Ajax* and *Achilles*, which were now approaching his port bow on a course of 340°. However, as *Exeter* closed the range and her 8in guns began firing full salvoes, Langsdorff concentrated both 11in turrets on her and quickly scored several hits. *Exeter* was now seriously damaged, with both forward turrets out of action, a fire raging amidships and most of her bridge staff killed or wounded, and was being conned from an emergency steering position right aft. Her after turret was in local control. Despite this, she manoeuvred to fire her port torpedoes, although these missed.

Seeing *Exeter*'s predicament, Harwood ordered his two light cruisers to close the range and they, in turn, came in for some punishment; *Achilles* suffered from a near miss while *Ajax* had her after turrets knocked out by an 11in shell. For a while, the light cruisers hauled off, but closed the range again when Langsdorff turned towards the crippled *Exeter* with the apparent intention of finishing her off. Fortunately, he turned away and after a few parting salvoes which brought down *Ajax*'s topmast and wireless aerials, he settled onto a westerly course with the two British light cruisers trailing him but keeping out of range. From the British point of view, the action was now in the balance. The *Exeter* was too seriously damaged to continue (her after turret had now failed) and she was instructed to make for the Falkland Islands for repairs. *Ajax* and *Achilles* were both damaged and had expended well over half their 6in ammunition. On the other hand, although declining action, the *Graf Spee* appeared relatively undamaged and could still be capable of sinking the British ships if the action was renewed.

Amazingly, apart from a few salvoes to keep the cruisers at bay, Langsdorff continued to retreat eastwards and eventually entered Montevideo harbour, just after midnight. Daylight inspection revealed that the *Graf Spee* had received around twenty direct hits, and had suffered additional damage from near misses and splinters. The 11in turrets were serviceable but much of the associated fire control equipment was damaged or destroyed and also one 5.9in secondary gun appeared to be out of action. The most serious issue was several underwater hits on the forward hull, which would have affected her seaworthiness. Nevertheless, the situation was still critical for Harwood and his two light cruisers. With the nearest British forces two days' steaming away, the odds were still in the Germans' favour if the *Graf Spee* was to sortie before reinforcements could arrive. Fortunately, the heavy cruiser HMS *Cumberland* arrived at 2200 on the 14th, having steamed 1,000 miles from the Falklands in thirty-four hours. Ashore, a diplomatic game was played to ensure that the *Graf Spee* was not permitted to depart from the neutral port until heavier reinforcements could arrive. However, at 1815 on the evening of 17 December, the *Graf Spee* left Montevideo and headed south-west for only 6 miles before stopping and offloading her remaining crew onto an accompanying German supply vessel. Within minutes, the once proud ship was rent apart by demolition charges in the magazines and she burned fiercely as she settled in the shallow waters. Kapitän Langsdorff and his crew were taken to Argentina, where he subsequently committed suicide. This victory was a major boost for the Royal Navy in the early stages of the war.

Although popularly referred to as a 'pocket battleship', the German designation for Graf Spee *and her sister ships was Panzerschiffe (armoured ship). This view of the ship was taken when she attended the 1937 Coronation Review at Spithead.* (NARA)

Graf Spee *under way in the English Channel in August 1939 as she sailed for her wartime deployment. Note the Arado Ar196 floatplane on the catapult and the quadruple torpedo tubes on the stern.* (AC)

HMS Exeter. *Her six 8in guns fired 200lb shells which were outclassed by the 1,100lb projectiles of the* Graf Spee*'s 11in (280mm) guns.* (NARA)

The Leander class cruiser HMS Ajax *was Commodore Harwood's flagship. Visible amidships is her Seafox spotter seaplane, which was launched early in the battle.* (AC)

Above: *HMS* Achilles, *sister ship to* Ajax. *At the time of the battle she formed part of the New Zealand Division of the Royal Navy. It was not until 1941 that the Royal New Zealand Navy was officially formed and the ship became HMNZS* Achilles. (NARA)

Left: *Although not arriving off Montevideo until the evening of 14 December, the 8in armed cruiser HMS* Cumberland *was a welcome reinforcement to Commodore Harwood as he waited to see if the* Graf Spee *would renew the battle.* (NARA)

The wreck of the Graf Spee *was closely inspected by Royal Navy experts who were particularly interested to find that the ship was equipped with a Seetakt radar whose antenna can be seen above the gunnery director and rangefinder. In fact, the ship was the first Kriegsmarine vessel to receive such equipment and this accounted for the accuracy of the* Graf Spee*'s opening salvoes.* (AC)

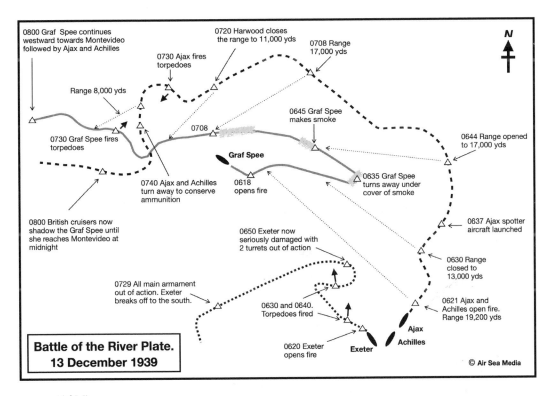

(ASM)

1st Battle of Narvik

Date:	10 April 1940
Location:	Ofotfjord, Narvik, northern Norway

Allied Forces

Commander:	Captain Bernard Armitage Warburton Warburton-Lee RN, Captain (D) 2nd Destroyer Flotilla
Ships:	Destroyers: *Hardy, Hunter, Hotspur, Havock, Hostile*

Axis Forces

Commander:	Commodore Friedrich Bonte, Officer Commanding Destroyers
Ships:	Destroyers: *Wilhelm Heidkamp, Georg Thiele, Wolfgang Zenker, Bernd von Arnim, Erich Giese, Erich Koellner, Diether von Roeder, Hans Lüdemann, Hermann Künne, Anton Schmitt*

BACKGROUND: On 9 April 1940, German forces moved to occupy Norway. The most northerly objective was Narvik, and the force assigned to this task consisted of ten modern destroyers under Commodore Bonte carrying between them a total of 2,000 troops. The battlecruisers *Scharnhorst* and *Gneisenau* would cover them as far as Vestafjord, a wide channel leading into the objective. The fast destroyers made rapid progress up the coast of Norway while snow showers and poor visibility protected them from patrolling British aircraft. Entering Ofotfjord on the morning of 9 April, they were able to reach their objective on schedule and began landing troops at various points around the fjord. Opposition from the Norwegian coast defence vessels *Eidsvold* and *Norge* was quickly smothered and both were sunk by torpedoes. By midday on the 9th, German troops were in complete control ashore. In the meantime, British forces already at sea had begun to wake up to what was happening and some skirmishes had already occurred. The battlecruiser HMS *Renown* had sighted the *Scharnhorst* and *Gneisenau* off the entrance to Vestafjord and a spirited action took place in which both of the German battlecruisers were damaged but managed to make good their escape to the north. Following this and having received reports of a German landing at Narvik, Vice Admiral Whitworth (British C-in-C) ordered Captain Warburton-Lee to detach a force of destroyers to investigate. He promptly set course with four destroyers of the 2nd Flotilla (later joined by a fifth destroyer) and planned to arrive at Narvik at 2000 on the evening of the 9th.

THE ACTION: In Narvik, Commodore Bonte was unable to leave as planned as his ships were short of fuel and an expected tanker had not arrived. The resulting delay was to cost him dear. Warburton-Lee's destroyers arrived in Vestafjord in the afternoon of the 9th but he decided to wait overnight and attack at dawn, setting course to reach the harbour at Narvik at 0430 on the morning of 10 April. Due to a misunderstanding, the German destroyer *von Roeder* had left her patrol position at the entrance to Ofotfjord just before the British destroyers arrived. Their passage was further aided by snow and mist, which hid them until the very last moment, when they achieved complete surprise on reaching the harbour at Narvik. In quick succession the destroyers *Heidkamp* and *Schmitt* were torpedoed and the *von Roeder* was heavily damaged by the concentrated gunfire of the British ships. Torpedoes launched from the *von Roeder* either missed or failed to explode.

After an hour, during which two other German destroyers were damaged by gunfire, Warburton-Lee decided to withdraw and set course westwards down the fjord. At this point they were intercepted by three more German destroyers (*Zenker*, *Giese* and *Koellner*) which had been moored overnight in Herjansfjord, which branched off to the north-east of Ofotfjord. Amazingly, it was almost forty-five minutes before they became aware of the commotion at Narvik and they barely managed to get steam up in time to chase the retiring British destroyers, who now worked up to 30 knots. In the running fight that developed, neither side scored any significant hits due to the poor visibility but, just as it seemed the British force would escape unscathed, they ran into the last two German destroyers (*Thiele* and *von Arnim*), which had now sortied from Ballengenfjord on the south side of the main channel. The leading ship, *Hardy*, was quickly hit by devastating 5in gunfire and a shell exploded on the bridge, mortally wounding Warburton-Lee and killing many others. With her steam lines cut and fierce fires raging, the ship was in danger of sinking, but one of the surviving officers managed to run her aground so that the crew could scramble ashore. Second in line was *Hunter*, which also received substantial damage and veered off course out of control. Behind her, *Hotspur* started to turn to avoid the damaged destroyer but an unlucky hit put her steering out of action and she ploughed into the stricken *Hunter*. Both ships now came under intense fire from all five German destroyers but eventually, *Hotspur* managed to free herself and limped away to the west. In the meantime, the two remaining British destroyers, *Havock* and *Hostile*, turned back and courageously engaged the superior German force, laying a smokescreen to assist the withdrawal of the damaged *Hotspur*. Fortunately, the German destroyers broke off the action at this point and retreated back to Narvik. The three remaining British destroyers now continued out to sea, leaving the *Hunter* sinking in mid-channel (all but fifty of her crew perishing) and *Hardy* burnt out ashore. In a parting shot, *Hostile* and *Havock* intercepted an inbound merchant ship, which proved to be the German *Rauenfels* carrying ammunition and supplies into Narvik. She was sunk by gunfire which triggered an enormous explosion.

Although the Royal Navy had lost two destroyers, the Germans had fared far worse. Of the ten German destroyers present, two were sunk and three (*von Roeder*, *Thiele* and *Arnim*) were so badly damaged that they were not capable of the voyage back to Germany. *Lüdemann* and *Künne* were also damaged and the remaining three had used up most of their ammunition. It was a brilliant victory for the British and Warburton-Lee was awarded a posthumous VC for his inspired leadership.

At the outbreak of war in September 1939, the Kriegsmarine possessed only twenty-two modern destroyers of the Maas and von Roeder classes, all armed with five 5in guns. (NARA)

The destroyer Hans Lüdemann *was refuelling in the harbour at Narvik, where she was surprised and badly damaged by the British destroyers.* (NARA)

The Georg Thiele *was the second Maas class destroyer to commission and was one of the German ships that were responsible for the destruction of the British destroyers* Hardy *and* Hunter. *However, she was seriously damaged, with two guns out of action and a magazine flooded.* (NARA)

The H class destroyer HMS Hunter *was one of two British destroyers lost in the first Narvik battle.* (ASM)

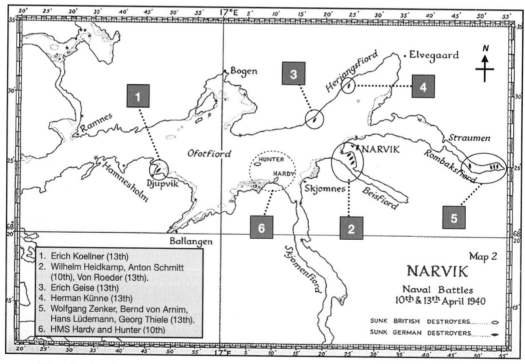

Map showing the location of ships sunk during the two Narvik battles on 10 and 13 April 1940. (ASM)

2nd Battle of Narvik

Date:	13 April 1940
Location:	Ofotfjord, Narvik, northern Norway

Allied Forces

Commander:	Vice Admiral William Jock Whitworth
Ships:	Battleship: *Warspite*. Destroyers: *Icarus, Hero, Foxhound, Forester, Kimberley, Bedouin, Punjabi, Eskimo, Cossack*

Axis Forces

Commander:	Kapitän Erich Bey, Commander 4th Destroyer Flotilla
Ships:	Destroyers: *Georg Thiele, Wolfgang Zenker, Bernd von Arnim, Erich Giese, Erich Koellner, Diether von Roeder, Hans Lüdemann, Herman Künne*. Submarine: *U-64*

BACKGROUND: Warburton-Lee's brave action with the 2nd destroyer flotilla had resulted in the remaining German destroyers being virtually stranded in Narvik due to lack of fuel, quite apart from the damaged state of some of the ships. However, several days passed before a decision was made to send a force into Ofotfjord to tackle the remaining destroyers. By 12 April, elements of the British Home Fleet had moved north to support the Narvik forces and an air strike of Swordfish aircraft was launched from the carrier *Furious* that evening, although this was unsuccessful. The following day, a major force would proceed via Vestafjord, through the narrows to Ofotfjord, with the objective of finishing off the trapped German destroyers.

THE ACTION: On the morning of 13 April, the British force made rendezvous in Vestafjord at 0730 and set course for Narvik, with some of the nine destroyers ahead streaming sweeps to counter a suspected minefield while others provided an anti-submarine screen for the battleship HMS *Warspite*. Kapitän Bey (who had taken over when Commodore Bonte had been killed on the 10th) had received advanced warning of the attack through the Germans' ability to read some of the British naval codes and prepared to disperse his ships in some of the side fjords, where they could perhaps surprise the approaching British ships. However, only the *Koellner* and *Künne* were actually got under way before the action and met the British force as it passed the narrows. The *Künne* raised the alarm and turned back to Narvik, while *Koellner* proceeded into Djupvik bay on the south side of the fjord in an attempt to hide. Both were sighted by the crew of HMS *Warspite*'s Swordfish floatplane, who immediately reported their positions before continuing up the fjord and spotting the disposition of the remaining six German destroyers. Turning north towards Herjansfjord, they surprised the submarine *U-64* on the surface and dived for an immediate attack, sinking her with two bombs. In the meantime, acting on warnings passed by the aircraft, the British destroyers successfully torpedoed the *Koellner*, which was finished off by a few 15in salvoes from *Warspite*.

Meanwhile, the retreating *Künne* had met up with the *Lüdemann*, *Zenker* and *Arnim* coming out of Narvik and together the four destroyers turned to meet the advancing British ships. A confused mêlée resulted, although the German ships slowly withdrew as their ammunition became depleted and eventually exhausted. Nevertheless, they had severely damaged *Punjabi*, which was out of action for nearly an hour and might well have sunk had it not been for the heroic efforts of her crew. In the midst of the fighting, ten Swordfish from HMS *Furious* attempted to bomb the German ships but only scored a few near misses for the loss of two aircraft.

As the battle swept up the fjord, the *Giese* emerged from the harbour at Narvik but was almost instantly overwhelmed by several British destroyers and was quickly reduced to a burning wreck. As *Cossack* then nosed into Narvik, she was met by accurate fire from the immobilised *von Roeder* berthed alongside the jetty and suffered substantial damage; her steering failed and she ran aground. Subsequently, the *von Roeder* blew up and sank, her crew having abandoned her after setting demolition charges. In the meantime, the last four German ships had retreated almost to the end of Rombaksfjord, past Narvik, where they were trapped and could go no further. *Thiele* was quickly hit and set on fire but managed to fire all her torpedoes before running onto rocks, where she capsized and sank. *Eskimo* was hit under the forecastle by one torpedo, which blew off the bow, although she continued in action and afterwards made it home for repairs. The remaining German vessels, *Lüdemann*, *Zenker* and *Arnim*, were abandoned and scuttled at the end of the fjord. This signalled the end of the action and the British force subsequently regrouped and withdrew, taking the damaged *Eskimo* and refloated *Cossack* with them. The victory was complete and in the two Narvik actions all ten German destroyers had been sunk.

The harbour at Narvik between the two battles. In the foreground is the Diether von Roeder *(Z17) with two more destroyers, one of which is* Wolfgang Zenker *(Z9). All three were sunk on 13 November.* (BA)

In the second Narvik battle, the British destroyers were backed up by the heavy guns of the battleship HMS Warspite. (NARA)

Warspite's *Fairey Swordfish proved to be extremely useful, providing warning of German destroyers hidden in side fjords and actually sinking the submarine* U-64 *with a pair of accurately placed bombs.* (NARA)

HMS Forester *was one of ten British destroyers deployed in the 2nd Narvik action.* (NARA)

The Tribal class destroyer HMS Eskimo *had her bow blown off during the action but managed to make it back to Britain after temporary repairs.* (NARA)

The upturned hulls of two sunken German destroyers pictured in Narvik harbour after the battle. (NHIC)

Loss of HMS *Glorious*

Date:	8 June 1940
Location:	Norwegian Sea, 250nm west of Narvik
Allied Forces	
Commander:	Captain Guy D'Oyly-Hughes DSO, DSC, RN
Ships:	Aircraft carrier: HMS *Glorious*. Destroyers: HMS *Ardent*, HMS *Acasta*
Axis Forces	
Commander:	Admiral Wilhelm Marschall
Ships:	Battlecruisers: *Scharnhorst*, *Gneisenau*

BACKGROUND: At the end of May 1940 it was decided that all 25,000 Allied troops would be evacuated from the Narvik area in two large convoys, the first of which sailed, almost unescorted, on 7 June followed by a second the following day. Among the vessels intended to cover this evacuation was the aircraft carrier HMS *Glorious*, which had been providing air support for the Narvik operations and, on the evening of the 7th, had flown on the remaining eighteen RAF fighters from airfields ashore. These included seven Hurricane monoplane fighters, a type whose performance had until that time precluded its operation from British aircraft carriers. As the RAF fighters did not have folding wings, their presence aboard the carrier somewhat restricted flying operations and this was one reason why *Glorious* was given permission to proceed independently to the UK, escorted only by the destroyers *Ardent* and *Acasta*, on the morning of 8 June.

On the German side, a task force consisting of the battlecruisers *Scharnhorst* and *Gneisenau*, together with the heavy cruiser *Hipper* and a number of destroyers, was assembled at Kiel and sailed on 4 June. Codenamed Operation Juno, the German sortie was intended to interrupt the flow of Allied ships to and from Norway, and to provide support for the German land forces still engaged in northern Norway. At that point the Germans were unaware of the Allied plan to evacuate Norway but by the 7th, Luftwaffe air reconnaissance had reported a significant westward movement of the British and French forces and the German ships were then ideally placed to intercept both convoys. On the morning of the 8th, the cruiser *Hipper* and the destroyers were detached to deal with one reported group of ships while the two battlecruisers turned north, intending to intercept the second convoy. It was late in the afternoon when, at 1545, a lookout aboard the *Scharnhorst* spotted smoke on the eastern horizon.

THE ACTION: Having successfully landed on the RAF fighters, HMS *Glorious* had turned for home and on the afternoon of the 8th was steaming at a leisurely 17 knots in a relaxed state of readiness, following a mean course of 250°. The two destroyers were stationed ahead of her but no one spotted the German ships passing ahead to the west until they turned onto an easterly course to close the range. At this moment they were sighted from *Glorious*, which turned away to the south while the engine room crew made every effort to raise steam in order to increase speed. On deck, frantic efforts were being made to arm and range a strike of Swordfish aircraft, but this took time as the aircraft were not at immediate readiness. At one point it appeared that *Glorious* might be outrunning the German ships and there was some possibility that she might escape, but at 1630, the battlecruiser's 11in guns were within range (28,000 yards) of *Glorious*. They began firing rapidly, scoring hits with only their third salvo, and at least one shell penetrated to the hangar deck, where it exploded and started a major fire. Aircraft on deck also caught fire and the bridge and superstructure was riddled. Initially she was able to maintain speed but damage to the boiler uptakes caused a drop in steam pressure and as the ship slowed down, the two battlecruisers caught up and were able to pound away until she rolled over and sank at 1810.

The two destroyers bravely attempted to defend the carrier and both laid a protective smokescreen. *Ardent* was much closer to the German ships when the action opened and managed to fire her torpedoes at *Gneisenau*, although these missed. She was then overwhelmed by the combined fire of the two battlecruisers' secondary batteries and sank at approximately 1728. The other destroyer, *Acasta*, had maintained station with *Glorious* until it was obvious that she was doomed. Her captain (Commander Charles Glasfurd) then turned back towards the enemy ships in a desperate attempt to stave off the inevitable. Dodging in and out of the smokescreen, Glasfurd skilfully handled his small destroyer and made two torpedo attacks before being eventually brought to a standstill as the result of several hits. The last torpedoes were fired at a range of 13,000 yards and one struck home on the *Scharnhorst*'s starboard side abreast the after 11in gun turret. This did considerable damage, killed forty-eight crew, and reduced her to 20 knots. The Germans continued to pour fire into the *Acasta*, which eventually sank around 1820. By then the action was over and the two battlecruisers set course away to the south-east. On the British side, the loss of the *Glorious* was not realised as the Germans had successfully jammed most of her radio transmissions. In fact, it was a triumphant broadcast by German radio that alerted the Admiralty, although even then there was no concentrated search for survivors, some of whom were eventually picked up by Norwegian merchant ships and trawlers. In all, some 1,500 men perished in this tragic incident.

HMS Glorious *had been heavily involved in the Norway campaign but on 8 June she was proceeding independently following the evacuation of Allied ground troops.* (NARA)

The powerful battlecruisers Scharnhorst *(foreground) and* Gneisenau *operating in company off the Norwegian coast.* (BA)

Scharnhorst's forward 11in guns in action against the Glorious. *The firing was incredibly accurate, scoring a hit at a range of over 26,000 yards with her third salvo.* (NHIC)

A pre-war view of HMS Acasta *bearing the funnel markings of the 3rd Destroyer Flotilla, to which she was assigned at the time. Although eventually sunk by the German battlecruisers, she scored a torpedo hit on the* Scharnhorst, *which caused substantial damage.* (AC)

A dramatic view from the Scharnhorst *showing the smokescreen being laid by the destroyer HMS* Acasta *to hide the* Glorious. Acasta *was later sunk but only after making a successful torpedo attack. (NHIC)*

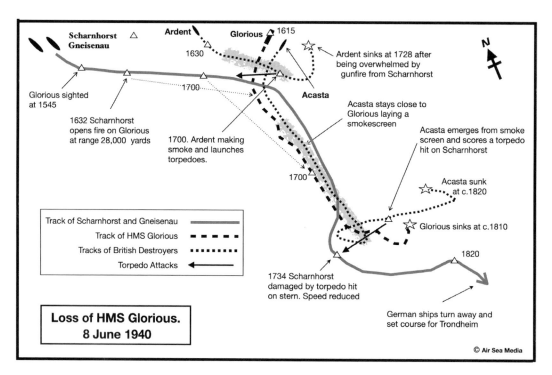

(ASM)

The Pursuit of the *Bismarck*

Date:	21 to 27 May 1941
Location:	48°04' north, 15°59' west (position of *Bismarck* sinking, approximately 400nm west of Brest)
Allied Forces	
Commander:	Admiral Sir John Tovey RN (C-in-C Home Fleet)
Ships:	Battleships: *King George V*, *Prince of Wales*, *Rodney*. Battlecruisers: *Hood*, *Repulse*. Aircraft Carrier: *Victorious*. Cruisers: *Norfolk*, *Suffolk*. Destroyers: *Cossack*, *Sikh*, *Maori*, *Zulu*, *Poirun*
Commander Force H:	Vice Admiral Sir James Somerville RN
Ships:	Battlecruiser: *Renown*. Aircraft carrier: *Ark Royal*. Cruiser: *Sheffield*
Axis Forces	
Commander:	Admiral Günther Lütjens
Ships:	Battleship: *Bismarck*. Heavy cruiser: *Prinz Eugen*

BACKGROUND: On 18 May 1941, the new 50,000-ton battleship *Bismarck* and heavy cruiser *Prinz Eugen* sailed through the Kattegat between Denmark and Sweden before proceeding north to the Norwegian port of Bergen with the intention of breaking out into the Atlantic to attack Allied convoys. Their passage from the Baltic was reported from Swedish sources and the two ships were located at Bergen by RAF reconnaissance aircraft on the afternoon of the 21st. At Scapa Flow, Admiral Tovey, C-in-C Home Fleet, immediately planned the deployment of ships to counter any possible foray by the German force into the North Atlantic. To the north, the cruisers *Norfolk* and *Suffolk* under Rear Admiral Wake-Walker patrolled the Denmark Strait between Iceland and the Arctic ice field. South of Iceland, covering the Faroes Gap, were the cruisers *Manchester*, *Birmingham* and *Arethusa*. The Admiralty also placed the battlecruiser *Repulse* and aircraft carrier *Victorious* at the disposal of the C-in-C, these ships having previously been scheduled to accompany a Gibraltar-bound convoy. Finally, the battlecruiser

Hood, the new battleship *Prince of Wales* and escorting destroyers were ordered northwards to assist Wake-Walker's force covering the Denmark Strait.

This powerful force left Scapa Flow at 0052 on the morning of the 22nd, although it was not until the evening that a Fleet Air Arm aircraft finally confirmed that the *Bismarck* and *Prinz Eugen* had left Bergen. They had actually sailed almost twenty-four hours earlier. Admiral Tovey immediately left Scapa Flow with the rest of the Home Fleet, including HMS *Victorious*, and set course to the west, where he would be in the best position to support the forces already deployed. 23 May passed slowly, with no news of the German ships until late in the evening when the cruiser *Suffolk* sighted the two German ships racing through the fog banks of the Denmark Strait. Sighting reports were immediately dispatched and the two cruisers settled down to shadow the enemy ships until heavier forces could be brought to bear. In fact, Admiral Tovey's dispositions had been remarkably effective and it was quickly apparent that Vice Admiral Holland's force (*Hood* and *Prince of Wales*) was ideally placed to intercept the *Bismarck* and *Prinz Eugen* early on the 24th to the south-west of Iceland. Accurate and effective reporting from the shadowing cruisers enabled Holland to bring his two capital ships into contact with the enemy at 0535, just as dawn was breaking.

LOSS OF HMS *HOOD*: Not wasting any time, Holland ordered the *Hood* and *Prince of Wales* onto a north-westerly course to close the enemy as quickly as possible. At 0552, *Hood* opened fire while *Bismarck* replied two minutes later with very accurate shooting. As the range fell to less than 20,000 yards, Holland ordered the *Hood* and *Prince of Wales* to turn to port in order to open the A arcs so that all guns could fire but, even as they did so, the *Bismarck*'s fifth salvo crashed home on the *Hood*. Within seconds, the great battlecruiser was rent apart by a massive explosion and sank within three minutes, leaving only a pall of smoke and three survivors from a crew of over 1,400 men. It was the Royal Navy's worst ever calamity. To make matters worse, the German ships quickly concentrated their fire on the *Prince of Wales*, which was hit several times. One shell landed directly on the bridge, killing or wounding most of the men stationed there. With her after turret jammed, she was forced to withdraw and the two German ships made off to the south-west, still doggedly shadowed by the cruisers *Norfolk* and *Suffolk*. Although not immediately realised, the *Bismarck* had not escaped unscathed, having been hit at least twice by heavy calibre shells. One of these had caused flooding in some of the bow compartments and ruptured vital fuel tanks, this damage subsequently restricting the ship to a maximum of 28 knots.

THE CHASE: The loss of the *Hood* now made it vital for the Royal Navy to sink the *Bismarck* if pride was to be restored. Throughout the 24th, more ships were ordered to join the hunt, including the battleships *Rodney*, *Ramillies* and *Revenge*, which had been escorting various convoys while Force H (*Ark Royal*,

Renown and *Sheffield*) was already heading north from Gibraltar. By the end of the day, as the *Bismarck* and *Prinz Eugen* headed south still shadowed by the British cruisers, there were five battleships, two battlecruisers, two aircraft carriers and twelve cruisers, as well as many destroyers actively involved in the operation. Among these was the carrier *Victorious*, which was ploughing steadily westwards in an attempt to get within range to launch an air strike. As her hangars were full of crated Hurricanes for delivery to Malta, she could only operate a small force of six Fulmars and nine Swordfish. Armed with torpedoes, the latter were launched late in the evening of the 24th and made a brave night attack through rain showers, claiming at least one hit.

By now the German battleship was alone, the *Prinz Eugen* having separated undetected before the air attack and eventually reached Brest on 1 June. In the meantime, the *Bismarck* continued south but, in the early hours of the 25th, she managed to shake off the cruisers, which had been following her for over thirty hours, and altered course to the south-east, heading towards Brest. The two cruisers, with the damaged *Prince of Wales* still in company, fanned out to the south-west and began to draw away from their prey. The next twenty-four hours were critical for the British forces as all resources were concentrated on relocating the *Bismarck* but, as the hours dragged by, there was a very real prospect that she would escape.

Unaware that contact had been lost, the *Bismarck* transmitted several long messages back to Germany, which were picked up by British D/F stations. Unfortunately these were incorrectly plotted and gave a false impression that she had reversed course and was heading back towards Norway. Admiral Tovey brought the *King George V* round onto a north-easterly course but by now the fuel state aboard many of the ships, which had been steaming at high speed for several hours, was becoming critical. The *Repulse* and several cruisers had to withdraw and others were forced to reduce speed. As time wore on, the Admiralty revised its appreciation of the situation in the light of an Ultra decode and a revised D/F plot, which indicated that *Bismarck* was still heading for France, and the C-in-C consequently turned back to the south.

Eventually, contact was regained at 1030 on the morning of the 26th by a Catalina flying boat of 209 Squadron, but by then the *Bismarck* was far ahead of the *King George V* and there was little chance of catching her. The only hope lay in the Swordfish torpedo aircraft aboard the carrier *Ark Royal*, which was ideally placed ahead of the *Bismarck*'s track. The first strike of fourteen aircraft was flown off at 1450 and, sighting a ship through the broken cloud, they dived to the attack and launched eleven torpedoes. Unfortunately, their target was not the *Bismarck* but the cruiser *Sheffield*, which had been detached to shadow the German battleship. Luckily, the torpedoes missed, although some exploded prematurely. A second strike was hastily arranged and, benefiting from experience, the torpedoes' duplex pistols were replaced by contact pistols.

This time there was no mistake and at 2053, fifteen Swordfish began their gallant attacks through heavy anti-aircraft fire, coming in close before dropping their torpedoes. At least two of these hit but initially it was difficult to ascertain what damage had been caused. In fact, one of the torpedoes had struck the starboard quarter, damaging the steering gear and jamming the rudders so that the ship began circling uncontrollably before eventually settling on a meandering course to the north-west.

THE FINAL ACTIONS: The way was now clear for the *King George V*, with the battleship *Rodney* now in company, to close and engage the *Bismarck*, but Tovey decided to hold off until dawn. In the meantime, the 4th Destroyer Flotilla (*Zulu, Sikh, Cossack, Maori, Poirun*) under Captain Vian had been detached from convoy WS.8B and was directed to harass the enemy through the night. This they did most successfully and at least two torpedo hits were claimed. Thereafter they continued to shadow the *Bismarck* until morning, when the *King George V* and *Rodney*, supported by the cruisers *Norfolk* and *Dorsetshire*, finally gained contact at 0843 on the morning of the 27th. *Rodney* opened fire at 0847, the *King George V* following almost immediately, while coincidently the *Bismarck* replied, initially firing at *Rodney*. For once, the British gunnery was as accurate as the Germans' and *Rodney* scored a hit with her third salvo, and further hits put the *Bismarck*'s fore turrets out of action.

As the range closed to 12,000 yards, the combatants passed on reciprocal courses so at 0916, the British ships turned northwards and further closed the range as the *Bismarck*'s fire slackened under the punishment she was receiving. Finally, at around 1005, the two battleships closed to within 3,000 yards, *Rodney* scoring a hit with one of her 24.5in torpedoes at this point. The *Bismarck* was now a blazing wreck and was obviously finished so, desperately short of fuel, the British battleships broke off the action and set course to the north-west, leaving the *Norfolk* and *Dorsetshire* to finish her off with torpedoes. The great German battleship rolled over and sank at 1040. The remaining British ships closed in to pick up survivors but only 110 were eventually rescued before it was necessary to withdraw under threat of possible aircraft and U-boat attacks. The *Hood* had been avenged and one of the greatest and most dramatic sea chases was at an end.

The cruiser HMS Suffolk *was the first to locate the* Bismarck *as she passed through the Denmark Strait.* (NARA)

Displacing over 50,000 tons at full load and armed with eight 15in guns, the Bismarck *would have wrought havoc amongst the British convoys if she had broken out into the expanses of the Atlantic.* (ASM)

Despite later improvements to her armour, HMS Hood *proved as vulnerable to plunging fire as had her predecessors at Jutland twenty-five years earlier and was sunk by* Bismarck's *fifth salvo.* (SVL)

Sent into battle while still not fully operational, HMS Prince of Wales *was forced to withdraw after suffering some damage and experiencing problems with her main armament turrets. However, she also registered at least two hits on the* Bismarck *and the resulting damage was enough to cause Lütjens to abandon the mission and head for Brest.* (NARA)

The newly commissioned carrier HMS Victorious *was drawn into the chase for the* Bismarck *and launched a strike of torpedo-armed Swordfish, which attacked just before midnight on 24 May, claiming at least one hit.* (WC)

Prior to the carrier attack, the cruiser Prinz Eugen *had been detached and eventually reached Brest on the evening of 1 June.* (ASM)

It was Swordfish from the carrier HMS Ark Royal *that sealed the* Bismarck's *fate when one of their torpedoes hit the stern and crippled the steering gear.* (ASM)

The cruiser HMS Sheffield *was the subject of a mistaken attack by the first wave of Swordfish. However, this revealed the fact that the magnetic pistols on their torpedoes were faulty and reliable contact pistols were fitted for the successful second strike.* (WC)

Above: *Admiral Tovey's flagship was HMS* King George V, *which, together with HMS* Rodney, *finally caught up with the* Bismarck *after a dramatic four-day chase.* (NARA)

Right: (ASM)

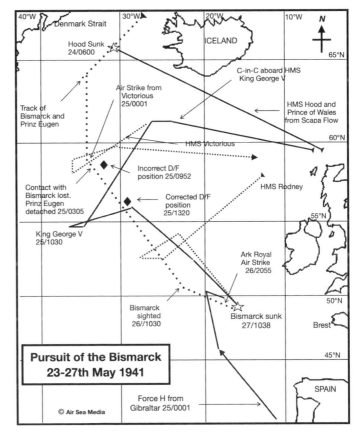

Denmark Strait

Hood Sunk
24/0600

ICELAND

C-in-C aboard HMS
King George V

HMS Hood and
Prince of Wales
from Scapa Flow

Air Strike from
Victorious
25/0001

Track of
Bismarck and
Prinz Eugen

HMS Victorious

Incorrect D/F
position 25/0952

Contact with
Bismarck lost.
Prinz Eugen
detached 25/0305

Corrected D/F
position
25/1320

HMS Rodney

King George V
25/1030

Ark Royal
Air Strike
26/2055

Bismarck
sighted
26//1030

Bismarck sunk
27/1038

Brest

**Pursuit of the Bismarck
23–27th May 1941**

© Air Sea Media

Force H from
Gibraltar 25/0001

SPAIN

40°W   30°W   20°W   10°W   N
65°N
60°N
55°N
50°N
45°N

Operation Cerberus – The Channel Dash

Date:	11 to 13 February 1942
Location:	English Channel and North Sea

Allied Forces

Flag Officer Dover:	Vice Admiral Sir Bertram Ramsey RN
Ships:	Destroyers: *Campbell*, *Vivacious* (21st destroyer flotilla), *Mackay*, *Worcester*, *Whitshed*, *Walpole* (16th destroyer flotilla). Minelayer: *Welshman*. Nine MTB/MGB
Aircraft:	Swordfish (825 NAS), Beaufort torpedo bombers (42, 86, 217 squadrons, RAF Coastal Command), approximately 250 aircraft of RAF Bomber Command

Axis Forces

Commander:	Vice Admiral Otto Ciliax
Ships:	Battlecruisers: *Scharnhorst*, *Gneisenau*. Cruiser: *Prinz Eugen*. Destroyers: *Z29*, *Z25*, *Richard Beitzen*, *Paul Jacobi*, *Friedrich Ihn*, *Hermann Schoemann*. Torpedo boats: *T2*, *T4*, *T5*, *T11*, *T12* (2nd TB flotilla), *T13*, *T15*, *T16*, *T17* (3rd TB Flotilla), *Seeadler*, *Falke*, *Kondor*, *Iltis*, *Jaguar* (5th TB Flotilla)
Aircraft:	176 bombers and fighters (Luftflotte 3)

BACKGROUND: Following a successful Atlantic sortie, the *Scharnhorst* and *Gneisenau* had arrived in Brest on 22 March 1941. On 1 June they were joined by the cruiser *Prinz Eugen*, which had been accompanying the *Bismarck* on her ill-fated voyage in late May. All three German ships were subjected to continuous heavy air attacks over the next few months and each received substantial damage. If they remained at Brest it was almost inevitable that they would eventually be sunk by bombing and, at Hitler's instigation, an audacious and detailed plan was drawn up to get them back to Germany. The chosen route was not over the vast expanses of the Atlantic Ocean, but through the narrow waters of the English Channel, right under the noses of the Royal Navy and the RAF. On paper it was an extremely risky operation and one that would almost certainly result in the loss of some of the ships attempting the passage. In fact, by a combination of planning, skill, determination and luck, the German ships were to score a major tactical success and severely embarrass the British at a critical time in the war.

THE PASSAGE: Luck was with Germans from the very start. The two battlecruisers, accompanied by the *Prinz Eugen* and the 5th Destroyer Flotilla were scheduled to leave Brest at 1930, although this was delayed for almost three hours due to an air raid alert. By the time the ships were at sea the RAF air patrols which might have located them were suffering from problems with their ASV radars and consequently their departure went undetected. In the forenoon, as the ships raced up the Channel at 28 knots, they were masked from further air reconnaissance by low cloud and rain and were joined by torpedo boat flotillas from Le Havre and, later, from Dunkirk. In addition, in a rare example of faultless co-operation between the Luftwaffe and the Kriegsmarine, a continuous escort of sixteen aircraft was stationed over the ships at all times. Thus it was not until 1042 that the ships were spotted already past Le Havre by a lone Spitfire, whose pilot did not make a sighting report until after landing back at his base at 1109. By then a radar plot of the German aircraft escorting the ships had already alerted naval staff and the British response was being prepared. In fact, the breakthrough of the German ships had been anticipated for some time and Operation Fuller, involving a co-ordinated response by surface ships, together with aircraft of Bomber and Coastal commands, had been planned in some detail. However, no one had anticipated a daylight attempt or that the German ships would ever get so far before being located and now time was very much of the essence.

The first force to react were five MTBs based at Dover, which left harbour at 1155 and immediately set course towards the enemy force, which was already approaching the narrowest part of the Dover Strait. Making contact at 1223, they were unable to penetrate the close escort of E-boats and torpedo boats and fired off their torpedoes at around 4,000 yards before withdrawing without loss. No hits were made but as they withdrew, six Swordfish of 825 Squadron, led by Lieutenant Commander Eugene Esmonde, swept in to attack. An expected escort of Spitfires had missed the rendezvous and the slow-moving biplanes were shot out of the sky by the German fighters or the intense AA fire of the ships. Again, no torpedo hits were obtained. Esmonde was awarded a posthumous VC for this brave but futile effort. MTBs from Ramsgate had also sortied but failed to engage. Shore batteries at Dover had briefly opened fire at 1215 but, by then, the German ships were rapidly moving out of range and no damage was done.

After the Swordfish attacks, the German force continued to head north-east for another two hours without further attacks, their progress uncontested until, at 1430, a shuddering explosion racked the *Scharnhorst* and she slowed to a stop off the Belgian coast. She had hit a mine but as it transpired was not badly damaged and was soon under way again. From about 1445 onwards, over a period of two and half hours, the German ships were subject to a series of uncoordinated air attacks by aircraft of Bomber Command and Beaufort torpedo bombers of Coastal Command. The solid cloud cover at around 1,500 feet frustrated most of these attacks and only thirty-nine bombers actually located their targets and some thirteen Beauforts pressed home torpedo attacks, but, in all this activity, no hits were scored and the German force ploughed steadily northwards.

The only other British forces able to intercept were the Harwich-based destroyers of the 21st and 16th flotillas. These were all First World War vintage destroyers and were already at sea off the East Anglian coast on exercise when they received a signal at 1156 informing the senior officer, Captain C.T.M. Pizey, that the enemy ships were proceeding up Channel. As the picture became clearer, it was apparent that he would only be able to intercept by proceeding eastwards over a known minefield, a course of action that Pizey accepted, although one of his ships, *Walpole*, had to turn back due to an engine defect. The other five, despite attacks by both enemy and friendly aircraft, eventually made contact with the German ships off the Hook of Holland at 1517. *Campbell* led *Vivacious* and *Worcester* to attack one of the battlecruisers while *Mackay* and *Whitshed* pressed on and launched torpedoes at a ship that turned out to be the *Prinz Eugen*. Throughout the attack, in which no hits were scored, the destroyers were subjected to heavy fire from all sides and *Worcester* was brought to a stop by several direct hits, and for some time was in danger of sinking. As the action swept past her, some temporary repairs were made and she eventually made it back to Harwich.

Apart from spasmodic and unsuccessful air attacks, nothing further could be done to stop the German ships, although the *Gneisenau* hit a mine at 1955 while north of Vlieland. However, damage was slight and she was soon under way again at 25 knots. Almost two hours later, at 2247, the *Scharnhorst* struck a second mine, which caused more serious damage than the first. All engines were stopped and she shipped 1,000 tons of water before the flooding was brought under control. Eventually she got under way again and limped into Wilhelmshaven the next morning. Almost certainly, these mines had been laid by aircraft of RAF Bomber Command on 11 February as a result of information obtained from Ultra decodes. Nevertheless, the outcome was an undoubted tactical victory for the German Navy, although in strategic terms little was actually gained. The *Gneisenau* was seriously damaged in a bombing raid only two weeks later and she was never again fit for service. The *Scharnhorst* went on to join German naval forces in Norway, but at least the Royal Navy could now concentrate its own forces to meet this threat without also having to guard against a breakout by other ships based on the French ports.

Above: *The battlecruiser* Scharnhorst *was the flagship of Vice Admiral Ciliax for Operation Cerberus. Despite striking two mines off the Dutch coast, the ship eventually reached Wilhelmshaven under her own steam.* (BA)

Right: Gneisenau, *sister ship to the* Scharnhorst, *also reached Germany safely but was later put out of action by RAF bombers.* (NARA)

The 5th Torpedo Boat Flotilla, which included the Seeadler, *shown here, joined the escort off Cap Gris-Nez. The Kriegsmarine commissioned numerous torpedo boats, which were, in effect, small destroyers but had no direct counterparts in the Royal Navy.* (NARA)

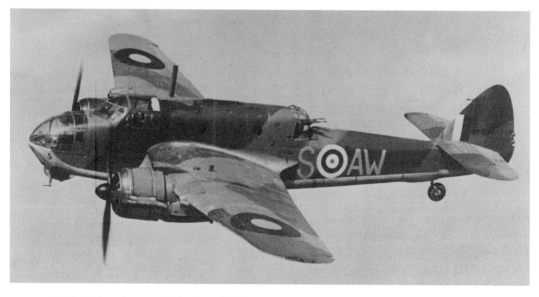

A Bristol Beaufort torpedo bomber of 42 Squadron, one of the units that mounted unsuccessful attacks against the German ships. (NARA)

HMS Campbell, *originally launched in 1918, was one of five Harwich-based vintage destroyers that made unsuccessful torpedo attacks in a last-ditch effort to stop the German ships.* (NARA)

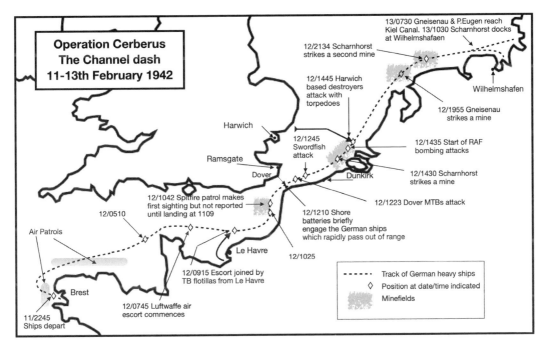

(ASM)

Convoy PQ17

Date:	27 June to 10 July 1942
Location:	Barents Sea, approximately 300 miles north of Norwegian coast

Allied Forces
Home Fleet

Covering Force:	Admiral John Cronyn Tovey RN
Ships:	Battleships: *Duke of York*, USS *Washington*. Aircraft carrier: *Victorious*. Cruisers: *Nigeria*, *Cumberland*. Fourteen destroyers

Home Fleet

Support Force:	Rear Admiral Louis Henry Keppel Hamilton RN
Ships:	Cruisers: *London*, *Norfolk*, USS *Tuscaloosa*, USS *Wichita*. Destroyers: *Somali*, *Rowan*, *Wainwright*

Convoy Escort

Commander:	Commander John 'Jack' Egerton Broome RN
Ships:	Destroyers: *Keppel*, *Offa*, *Fury*, *Leamington*, *Ledbury*, *Wilton*. Corvettes: *Lotus*, *Poppy*, *Dianella*, *La Malouine*. AA ships: *Palomares*, *Pozarica*. Four A/S trawlers. Submarines: *P614*, *P615*

Axis Forces

Operational Commander Group North (Kiel):	Admiral Rolf Hans Wilhelm Karl Carls
Flag Officer Narvik (responsible for U-boat operations):	Admiral Hubert Schmundt

Fleet Commander and Commander Force I:	Admiral Otto Schniewind
Ships (Force I):	Battleship: *Tirpitz*. Cruiser: *Admiral Hipper*. Destroyers: *Karl Galster, Friedrich Ihn, Hans Lody, Theodor Riedel*. Torpedo boats: *T7, T15*
Commander Force II:	Vice Admiral Oskar Kummetz
Ships (Force II):	Armoured ships: *Lützow, Admiral Scheer*. Destroyers: *Richard Beitzen, Z24, Z27, Z28, Z29, Z30*
Other forces:	Several U-boats including *U-88, U-251, U-255, U-334, U-376, U-456, U-457, U-657, U-703*. Aircraft of Luftflotte V including He 111 torpedo bombers (KG26) and Ju 88 dive-bombers (KG30)

BACKGROUND: In June 1941, Germany attacked Russia and the British Government subsequently decided to instigate supply convoys from Britain to the ports of Murmansk and Archangel on the north-west Russian coast. The first convoy of seven merchant ships sailed in August 1941 and reached Archangel without loss. Thereafter, convoys to and from the UK sailed regularly through the winter. Losses were light and the main enemy was the weather. However, convoy PQ13, which sailed in February 1942, met stiff resistance, losing five merchant ships to attacks by submarine, aircraft and surface forces. The next convoy, PQ14, lost only one ship but two thirds of the merchantmen turned back due to extreme weather conditions. PQ15 lost three ships to air attack and PQ16 was mauled by air and submarine attacks. The returning convoys fared little better and several merchant ships as well as a cruiser and a number of smaller warships were lost. The next northbound convoy, PQ17, was ready to sail in late June 1942, at the height of the summer, when the Arctic days were at their longest. If it was to have any chance of getting through, it would need a very strong escort and more than its fair share of luck. The stage was set for one of the greatest disasters of the war

THE ACTION: The protection of PQ17 was on now well-established lines. The convoy itself would have a close escort of six destroyers, four corvettes and four anti-submarine trawlers, together with two merchant ships which had been converted to AA escorts. A support force of four cruisers would operate in the vicinity of the convoy while a distant covering force, which included the aircraft carrier HMS *Victorious* and two battleships (one British and one American), would intervene if the convoy was threatened by German heavy units, particularly the powerful battleship *Tirpitz*. Apart from the close escort, the other covering forces were not expected to proceed beyond Bear Island, where they could be subject to sustained air attack, although substantial numbers of British and Russian submarines were deployed as a counter to any sortie by the German capital ships.

PQ17 sailed in good order on 27 June and consisted initially of some thirty-seven merchant ships, of which around two thirds were American. Despite the good weather, it was not sighted by German reconnaissance aircraft until 1 July. That evening, a small-scale torpedo attack by He 115 floatplanes was beaten off with no loss and thick fog prevented further attacks for most of the following two days. Attempts by various U-boats to attack the convoy on the 3rd were repelled by the close escort and no air attacks developed, although early the following day a single He 115 made a successful attack and torpedoed the *Christopher Newport*, which later sank after most of her crew had been rescued. That evening, two much stronger attacks developed, although the first was unsuccessful. Half an hour later, twenty-five He 111s of KG26 pressed home a determined attack and sank one freighter and damaged two others, one of which was subsequently finished off by *U-334*. Three aircraft were shot down. Up to this point, things were going reasonably well for the convoy and its escort and there was every confidence that further attacks could be contained and losses kept at an acceptable level.

Following the sighting of the convoy, Group North ordered the *Lützow* and *Scheer* with six destroyers to leave Narvik for Altenfjord at the northern tip of Norway (*Lützow* subsequently ran aground and took no further part in the operation). In the meantime, *Tirpitz* and *Hipper* left Trondheim and headed north to rendezvous with the other force. British efforts to monitor German ships had been hampered by the same foggy conditions that had protected the convoy and it was not until 3 July that an RAF aircraft reported that the *Tirpitz* was not at Trondheim. Further reconnaissance failed to locate her, or the other German ships, and this caused mounting concern in London. From there, it appeared that the *Tirpitz* was loose in the Barents Sea and could fall on the convoy at any moment. The First Sea Lord, Sir Dudley Pound, convened a meeting with his staff to discuss the options. After some deliberation, it was decided that heavy forces could not be risked east of Bear Island and that the convoy should be dispersed to reduce the number of available targets if the *Tirpitz* should come upon the scene.

At 2200 a signal was sent to Rear Admiral Hamilton: 'Most Immediate, Cruiser Force withdraw to westward at high speed.' This was followed by a further signal to the convoy: 'Immediate, owing to threat of surface ships, convoy is to disperse and proceed to Russian ports.' These signals were a bombshell, both to Hamilton and Commander Broome of the close escort. They could only assume that London had accurate information that enemy forces were in their immediate vicinity and that a surface action was imminent. This impression was heightened by a further signal received a few minutes later: 'Convoy is to scatter!' In the absence of any other specific orders, Broome rounded up his destroyers and steamed to join up with Hamilton's cruisers in order to support them in the anticipated action. As time passed, the slow realisation dawned that there was no enemy force in the vicinity but after several hours had elapsed, the scattering of the convoy meant that there was no possibility that the ships could be rounded up and reformed.

In the meantime, the Germans could scarcely believe their luck when they discovered early the following morning what had happened. On receipt of reports from aircraft and U-boats, the *Tirpitz*, accompanied by *Hipper*, *Scheer* and seven destroyers, left Altenfjord, where they had been lying undetected, and set course to hunt down the fleeing merchant ships. By this time every available aircraft and U-boat was heading towards the area and quickly and efficiently began to take a dreadful toll of the defenceless ships, sinking or damaging fourteen during the day. It quickly became apparent that the surface force was not required and it was ordered to break off and return to base. Nevertheless, the *Tirpitz*, by her mere presence and potential, had been the instrument of a major success for the German forces without herself firing a single shot.

The grim story continued over the next few days as other ships were sunk, although there were many instances of heroism and initiative amongst the few that survived, the last not reaching port until 28 July. The statistics made grim reading. Out of thirty-three ships which comprised the convoy (four others having turned back due to various problems), no less than twenty-four, totalling 142,695grt, were sunk. This was a major victory for the German forces and it resulted in the immediate suspension of Russian convoys for the rest of the summer. In addition, the Royal Navy had suffered a rare and resounding defeat which was to tarnish its reputation for many years to come.

The mere presence of the battleship Tirpitz *in northern Norway required significant diversion of naval resources to cover the important Arctic convoys such as PQ17. (AC)*

The USS Washington *(BB56) was one of several US Navy warships attached to the covering force for PQ17 along with Royal Navy ships including HMS* Victorious, *seen here in the background.* (NARA)

The Hunt class escort destroyer HMS Ledbury *was part of the convoy's close escort.* (NARA)

The close support force of four heavy cruisers was accompanied by four destroyers. One of these was the USS Wainwright *(DD419), which successfully broke up an air attack on 4 July and claimed one Ju.88 shot down.* (NARA)

After the convoy had scattered, the waiting U-boats had a field day and took a dreadful toll of the now undefended merchant ships. (NHIC)

U-225 (a Type VIIC U-boat) returns to base flying pennants signifying the four PQ17 merchant ships she had sunk. She also has the ensign taken from the SS Paulus Potter, *which was boarded after having been abandoned following an air attack and was then finished off with a torpedo.* (NHIC)

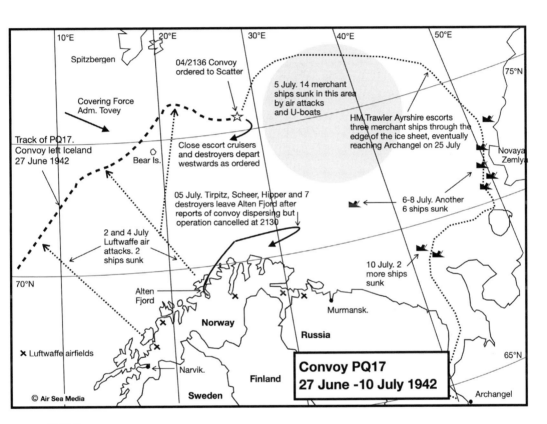

(ASM)

Battle of the Barents Sea

Date:	31 December 1942
Location:	Barents Sea, 200 miles NNE of North Cape, Norway

Allied Forces

Commander, close escort:	Rear Admiral Robert Lindsay Burnett RN
Ships:	Cruisers: *Jamaica*, *Sheffield*
Commander, convoy escort:	Captain Robert St Vincent Sherbrooke RN
Ships:	Destroyers: *Onslow*, *Obedient*, *Orwell*, *Obdurate*, *Oribi*, *Achates*. Corvettes: *Rhododendron*, *Hyderabad*. Minesweeper: *Bramble* and two A/S trawlers

Axis Forces

Commander:	Vice Admiral Oskar Kummetz
Ships:	Panzerschiffe: *Lützow*. Cruiser: *Admiral Hipper*. Destroyers: *Friedrich Eckholdt*, *Richard Beitzen*, *Theodor Riedel*, *Z29*, *Z30*, *Z31*

BACKGROUND: After the PQ17 disaster, the next convoy (PQ18) did not sail until 2 September and was the most heavily protected to date. Despite this, it had one of the hardest passages of any Russian convoy and ultimately lost no fewer than thirteen ships out of a total of forty, most to air attack. A return convoy, QP14, was run at the same time and lost three out of fifteen merchant ships. Given this scale of losses, the next convoy (JW51) was not scheduled until mid-December, when the longer nights and winter weather would afford additional protection. Some thirty merchant ships were assembled but it was decided to split them into two smaller and more manageable convoys designated JW51A and JW51B. The convoy escort was reinforced by two light cruisers, *Sheffield* and *Jamaica*, under Rear Admiral R.L. Burnett, and these were ordered to remain in the vicinity of the convoy east of Bear Island and all the way to the Kola Inlet. Distant support was provided by units of the Home Fleet under the C-in-C, Admiral Tovey. On the German side, although many aircraft were withdrawn from Norway where their use in the winter conditions was limited, there were numerous U-boats as well as the pocket battleship *Lützow* and heavy cruiser *Admiral Hipper* based at Altenfjord, from where they could sortie at short notice.

THE ACTION: JW51A sailed from Loch Ewe on 15 December 1942, and JW51B followed seven days later. The former had an unexpectedly quiet passage and reached the Kola Inlet safely on Christmas Day. JW51B also made good progress initially with its close escort under the command of Captain R. St V. Sherbrooke. On 28 December, the convoy was hit by a storm which caused some of the merchantmen to become detached and the minesweeper *Bramble* was sent to search for them. By New Year's Eve, the storm had blown itself out although being midwinter, full daylight was never attained and visibility varied between 4 and 10 miles, reducing in frequent snow showers. Following a U-boat sighting report, the *Lützow* and *Hipper*, together with six destroyers, had left Altenfjord on the evening of the 30th. Admiral Kummetz planned to deploy *Hipper* and three destroyers to the north of the convoy to engage and draw off the escorting destroyers. The *Lützow* and three more destroyers would then come at the convoy from the south and sink the merchant ships while the escort was otherwise engaged. Initially everything went well, with the *Hipper* passing astern of the convoy at around 0715 on the morning of the 31st. Sighting some ships in the distance, *Eckholdt* and two other destroyers were sent to investigate. These in turn were later sighted from HMS *Obdurate*, which was ordered to close and report, although it was not until 0930 that she was close enough to confirm their identity, at which point the German destroyers opened fire. Aboard the *Onslow*, Captain Sherbrooke immediately ordered *Orwell* and *Obedient* to join him and set off towards the sound of the guns. In the meantime, Kummetz ordered the *Hipper* to turn towards the convoy and to engage the *Achates*, which was now frantically laying a smokescreen across the rear of the convoy. As the *Hipper* turned she was spotted from *Onslow*, which, together with *Orwell*, immediately opened fire at a range of 5 miles, causing the cruiser to turn away to avoid a possible torpedo attack.

For a while Sherbrooke successfully held the *Hipper* at bay and, with some intuition of the German plan, ordered *Obedient* and *Obdurate* to return to cover the convoy. In the half-light and intermittent visibility, a cat and mouse game continued for a while until the *Hipper* eventually turned on the two remaining British destroyers and scored four hits on *Onslow*, causing severe damage and seriously wounding Sherbrooke. Meanwhile, Rear Admiral Burnett's two cruisers were to the north of the convoy although, due to radio silence being maintained, Burnett was not sure of its exact position and believed it to be further to the east. When he received Sherbrooke's sighting report, he also had radar contact with some unidentified ships to the north-east and initially headed towards them until it was realised that they were probably stragglers from the convoy. At the same time, the sight and sound of gunfire to the south increased and he therefore turned towards the source, working up to 31 knots. At around 1030, some radar contacts were picked up and shortly afterwards more gunfire erupted to the south, although it transpired that this was the *Hipper* dispatching the lone minesweeper *Bramble*, which had strayed into the path of the action. *Sheffield* had a brief visual contact with the *Hipper*, which was then lost from sight as she headed south and then east, aiming again for the convoy. As she did so, the destroyer *Achates* suddenly emerged from the drifting smokescreen and was hammered at point-blank range by the 8in guns of the *Hipper*. The gallant destroyer drifted away, to capsize and sink after the action, although eighty-one of her crew were rescued.

The *Hipper* now turned north-west and engaged the other British destroyers, but this turn took her straight into the path of the *Sheffield* and *Jamaica* coming down from the north. With the advantage of the light, they were able to open rapid fire and got off several salvoes before the German cruiser was able to reply. The *Hipper* was hit several times and one boiler room was put out of action, reducing her speed. As the cruisers slugged it out at ranges down to 4 miles, two German destroyers suddenly appeared out of the gloom heading for the *Sheffield*, which they had mistakenly thought to be the *Hipper*. *Sheffield*'s captain immediately sized up the situation and turned towards the destroyers, pouring a withering fire into the *Eckholdt*, and this was followed up by more of the same from the *Jamaica*, turning her into a blazing wreck. However, this distraction enabled the *Hipper* to turn away and eventually make good her escape to the west.

At 1137, Kummetz ordered the remaining German forces to break off the battle and withdraw. During all this time the *Lützow* had been hovering to the south-east of the convoy but, apart from briefly engaging a few ships at long range and damaging the destroyer *Obdurate*, her captain lacked the resolution to take advantage of the situation and quickly withdrew when ordered. As the *Lützow* headed west she was briefly engaged by the British cruisers but the German ships continued to withdraw and the action was over by 1236. JW51B was now safe and eventually reached the Kola Inlet without further loss.

When Hitler received the reports of the battle he was furious and the resulting restrictions under which German warships subsequently operated were almost enough to ensure that they would never again have such a good opportunity to destroy one of the British convoys. For the British it was a confidence-boosting victory after the fiasco of PQ17 and Captain Sherbrooke was awarded the VC for his courageous leadership of the destroyers.

The heavy cruiser Admiral Hipper *was the flagship of the German Vice Admiral Kummetz for Operation Regenbogen, the attack on convoy JW51B.* (NARA)

The Lützow *(originally* Deutschland *but renamed in 1940) was deployed as the other half of a trap to envelop the convoy in a pincer movement. However, despite being armed with heavy 11in guns, her captain was hesitant to close the convoy and only succeeded in damaging the destroyer* HMS *Obdurate.* (NARA)

The convoy's close escort included five newly commissioned O class destroyers, some of which (including HMS Obedient *shown here) were armed with 4in guns in lieu of the standard 4.7in guns in order to improve the ships' AA capabilities.* (NARA)

The intervention of the cruisers HMS Sheffield *and* Jamaica *(shown here) proved to be the turning point in the battle. Their quick-firing 6in guns proved more than a match for the the slower firing but heavier 8in guns of the* Admiral Hipper. (ASM)

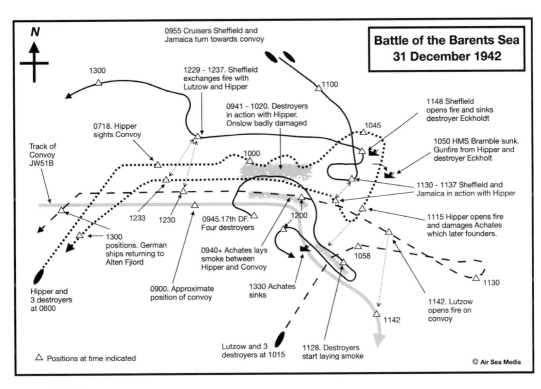

Battle of the Barents Sea
31 December 1942

N

0955 Cruisers Sheffield and Jamaica turn towards convoy

1300

1229 - 1237. Sheffield exchanges fire with Lutzow and Hipper

0941 - 1020. Destroyers in action with Hipper. Onslow badly damaged

1100

1148 Sheffield opens fire and sinks destroyer Eckholdt

0718. Hipper sights Convoy

1045

1050 HMS Bramble sunk. Gunfire from Hipper and destroyer Eckholt

Track of Convoy JW51B

1000

1130 - 1137 Sheffield and Jamaica in action with Hipper

1233   1230

0945.17th DF. Four destroyers

1200

1115 Hipper opens fire and damages Achates which later founders.

1300 positions. German ships returning to Alten Fjiord

0940+ Achates lays smoke between Hipper and Convoy

1058

1130

0900. Approximate position of convoy

1330 Achates sinks

1142. Lutzow opens fire on convoy

Hipper and 3 destroyers at 0600

1142

Lutzow and 3 destroyers at 1015

1128. Destroyers start laying smoke

△ Positions at time indicated

© Air Sea Media

(ASM)

Battle of North Cape

Date:	26 December 1943
Location:	Barents Sea, 100 miles north of North Cape, Norway
Allied Forces	
C-in-C Home Fleet, Commander Force 2:	Admiral Sir Bruce Fraser RN
Ships:	Battleship: *Duke of York*. Cruiser: *Jamaica*. Destroyers: *Savage, Scorpion, Saumarez,* H.No.M.S. *Stord*
Commander Force 1:	Vice Admiral Robert Lindsay Burnett RN
Ships:	Cruisers: *Belfast, Norfolk, Sheffield*. Destroyers: *Musketeer, Matchless, Opportune, Virago* (36th Destroyer Division)
Axis Forces	
Commander:	Rear Admiral Erich Bey
Ships:	Battlecruiser: *Scharnhorst*. Destroyers: *Z29, Z30, Z33, Z34, Z38*

BACKGROUND: On 20 December, convoy JW55B had left Loch Ewe, its passage coinciding with the homebound RW55A, which sailed from the Kola Inlet on 23 December 1943. The two convoys crossed in the vicinity of Bear Island on Christmas Day. While RW55A had not been detected, JW55B had been located and shadowed by U-boats and aircraft from the 22nd. By 0400 on the morning of the 26th, JW55B was some 50 miles south of Bear Island, heading east with a close escort under the command of Captain McCoy (D17) of no less than fourteen destroyers, two frigates and a minesweeper. Vice Admiral Burnett's cruiser covering force was some 150 miles to the east of the convoy but on a reciprocal course to close. The C-in-C with the battleship *Duke of York* was some 350 miles to the south-west but on a parallel course to the convoy. A German force consisting of the *Scharnhorst* and five destroyers had left Altenfjord on the previous evening and was heading north with the intention of attacking the convoy. News that the battlecruiser was at sea was confirmed by an Ultra report, on receipt of which Admiral Fraser had begun deploying his ships in an attempt to intercept the German ships. By 0800, the *Scharnhorst* had turned back onto a south-westerly course and was still attempting to locate the convoy when some 45 minutes later she was detected by Burnett's Force 1 approaching from the south-east.

THE ACTION: The British cruisers manoeuvred to close the range and *Norfolk* opened fire with her 8in guns on the *Scharnhorst*, obtaining two hits, one of which damaged the German ship's radar. As the *Scharnhorst* manoeuvred to escape this attack, her destroyers continued to the south-west and became detached, playing no further part in the day's events. The weather conditions were very rough (wind force 7–8) and the *Scharnhorst* was better able to maintain speed than the cruisers. She eventually drew away, steering to the north-east in an attempt to get around them and attack the convoy. Contact was lost for a while but Admiral Fraser ordered Captain McCoy and four destroyers of the 36th Division (*Musketeer, Matchless, Opportune, Virago*) to leave the convoy and reinforce the cruisers of Force 1 as they took up station 10 miles ahead of JW55B, ready for any further attack.

There was now a lull of almost two hours before the *Scharnhorst* was again detected on radar approaching from the east. At 1221 she was within range and the British cruisers opened fire, the *Scharnhorst* replying with her 11in guns. However, the combined firepower of the three light cruisers, supported by four destroyers, was enough to frustrate the *Scharnhorst*'s efforts to get at the convoy and she therefore turned away to the south with the intention of returning to Altenfjord, some 200 miles away. As the battlecruiser made off at high speed, the cruisers followed astern, reporting her movements to the C-in-C who, approaching in the *Duke of York* with *Jamaica* and four destroyers in company from the south-west, was now ideally placed to intercept. At 1617, radar contact was gained and as the range steadily closed, the destroyers were deployed ahead of the battleship in preparation for a torpedo attack. It was not until the range had closed to 12,000 yards that the *Duke of York*'s 14in guns opened fire on the *Scharnhorst*, which until that moment had been totally unaware of her dangerous situation. She immediately altered course to the east and a stern chase developed with the range slowly increasing as the German ship made the most of her speed advantage over the British battleship. The *Duke of York* obtained several hits on the *Scharnhorst*, one of which disabled the forward 11in gun turret, but her speed was unaffected and the two ships continued to fight it out. It was not until 1820, when the *Scharnhorst* suddenly appeared to slow down, probably as the result of a 14in hit, that the pursuing British destroyers were able to close the range and launch their torpedoes. At least four hits were obtained and the *Scharnhorst*'s fate was sealed, although she continued to fight against the increasingly overwhelming odds.

The *Duke of York* and *Jamaica* now closed the range and pounded the burning battlecruiser with numerous salvoes, while *Norfolk* and *Belfast* approaching from the north-west were also able to join in. By now the *Scharnhorst* had slowed to less than 5 knots and was a sitting target for further torpedo attacks by the 36th Destroyer Division and at least five hits were obtained. *Jamaica* also fired torpedoes and scored another two hits. The *Scharnhorst*, obscured by smoke and flames, was clearly finished and the British ships stood off as she eventually sank at around 1945. Despite an intensive search, only thirty-six survivors were rescued from a crew of almost 2,000 men, including forty cadets who had been embarked for training.

The battlecruiser Scharnhorst *ploughs through heavy seas, similar conditions to those pertaining on 26 December 1943 when a force 8 gale was blowing.* (ASM)

The heavy cruiser HMS Norfolk, *part of the covering force for convoy JW55B, was the first to engage the* Scharnhorst *and was present nearly twelve hours later when the German ship was finally sunk.* (ASM)

HMS Duke of York *was the flagship of Admiral Sir Bruce Fraser, and her 14in guns, firing under radar control, were instrumental in bringing the German battlecruiser to bay.* (NARA)

HMS Savage *was one of four S class destroyers which made the first torpedo attacks on the* Scharnhorst, *sealing the battlecruiser's fate with four hits.* Savage *differed from her sister ships in that she acted as trials ship for the 4.5in gun (replacing the usual 4.7in guns), which later became the standard destroyer armament. Notable is that the forward guns are mounted in a twin turret of a type later fitted to the Battle class destroyers.* (NARA)

Armed with twelve 6in guns, HMS Belfast *was part of the convoy covering force and, in company with* Norfolk, *was responsible for shadowing the* Scharnhorst *until she was intercepted by the* Duke of York *and accompanying destroyers.* (ASM)

Right: *Admiral Sir Bruce Fraser addressing the ship's company aboard HMS* Duke of York, *only a few weeks before the Battle of North Cape.* (NARA)

Below: (ASM)

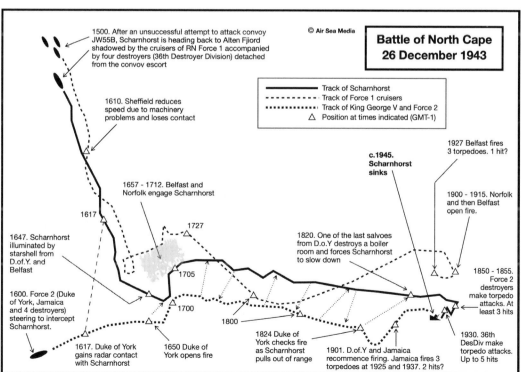

© Air Sea Media

**Battle of North Cape
26 December 1943**

───── Track of Scharnhorst
– – – – Track of Force 1 cruisers
▪▪▪▪▪▪▪ Track of King George V and Force 2
△ Position at times indicated (GMT-1)

1500. After an unsuccessful attempt to attack convoy JW55B, Scharnhorst is heading back to Alten Fjiord shadowed by the cruisers of RN Force 1 accompanied by four destroyers (36th Destroyer Division) detached from the convoy escort

1610. Sheffield reduces speed due to machinery problems and loses contact

1657 - 1712. Belfast and Norfolk engage Scharnhorst

1617

1727

1647. Scharnhorst illuminated by starshell from D.of.Y. and Belfast

1705

1600. Force 2 (Duke of York, Jamaica and 4 destroyers) steering to intercept Scharnhorst.

1700

1800

1617. Duke of York gains radar contact with Scharnhorst

1650 Duke of York opens fire

1824 Duke of York checks fire as Scharnhorst pulls out of range

1820. One of the last salvoes from D.o.Y destroys a boiler room and forces Scharnhorst to slow down

1901. D.of.Y and Jamaica recommence firing. Jamaica fires 3 torpedoes at 1925 and 1937. 2 hits?

c.1945. Scharnhorst sinks

1927 Belfast fires 3 torpedoes. 1 hit?

1900 - 1915. Norfolk and then Belfast open fire.

1850 - 1855. Force 2 destroyers make torpedo attacks. At least 3 hits

1930. 36th DesDiv make torpedo attacks. Up to 5 hits

Battle of the Atlantic

<table>
<tr><td>Date:</td><td>3 September 1939 to 8 May 1945</td></tr>
<tr><td>Location:</td><td>Atlantic Ocean</td></tr>
</table>

Allied Commanders

Royal Navy:	C-in-C Western Approaches: Admiral Sir Percy Noble RN (1939–42), Admiral Sir Max Horton RN (1942–45)
US Navy:	C-in-C Atlantic Fleet (CINCLANT): Admiral Royal Eason Ingersoll USN (1941–45), Admiral Jonas Howard Ingram USN (1945)

Axis Commander

C-in-C U-boats:	Admiral (later Grand Admiral) Karl Doenitz (appointed C-in-C German Navy 30 January 1943)

BACKGROUND: The Battle of the Atlantic was the longest naval battle in history and was fought almost continuously through five and half years of war. At stake initially was the very survival of Britain and its ability to resist the seemingly unstoppable German advances throughout Europe. Subsequently it was vital to protect the transatlantic shipping routes bringing across masses of men and materiel from America so that Germany could eventually be defeated. The campaign to defeat the U-boats was long and arduous and relied heavily on the application of scientific advances to introduce new weapons and operational methods. As well as being the longest battle, it was also the one that Britain and its allies could not afford to lose.

THE OPENING ROUNDS: The Royal Navy introduced a convoy system for merchant shipping as soon as war broke out. First World War experience had shown that this was the most effective way of reducing losses from submarine attack even though there was a woeful shortage of suitable escort ships. Fortunately, the Germans were equally short of U-boats, with only some forty-four actually ready for service, and only a few of these could actually be on patrol at any given moment. Nevertheless, by the end of 1939 they had sunk 114 merchantmen for the loss of only nine U-boats, and in the first half of 1940, they sank another 186 merchant ships while losing only fourteen U-boats. Although serious, these losses could be sustained by the British, but they were finding that sinking U-boats was turning out to be much more difficult than had been thought. During the interwar period, the Royal Navy had developed Asdic (later known as sonar), which appeared to be effective at locating submarines, and it was expected that destroyers and sloops equipped with this device would be able to counter the U-boat threat. However, the Germans easily countered this by attacking at night on the surface and, even if detected when submerged, it proved very difficult for an escort to make an accurate depth charge attack. In practice most successful actions at this stage of the war relied to some extent on luck.

HARD TIMES: The fall of France in mid-1940 dramatically altered the situation in favour of the German U-boats, which could now operate from the Atlantic ports of Brest, Lorient, St Nazaire and La Rochelle as well as from bases in Norway. Fw.200 Condor long-range bombers could patrol far over the Atlantic from bases in France and Norway to locate and shadow convoys, well out of range of Allied air patrols. Although the total number of operational U-boats was actually less than September 1939, Allied merchant ship losses began to rise alarmingly, totalling 2.4 million tons (577 ships) in the second half of 1940. In 1941, some 875 Allied ships, totalling 3.3 million tons, were lost and the operational U-boat fleet had grown from around thirty at the start of the year to over eighty. However, there were some encouraging signs for the Allies, who sank thirty-five U-boats in the year and, significantly, over half of these were achieved in the last four months, with ten being sunk in December alone. There were several factors to account for these successes, such as the availability of more escort vessels including fifty old ex-US destroyers supplied at the end of 1940, as well as new construction corvettes and converted V&W class destroyers. Moreover, a few of these ships were now being fitted with radar, which allowed submarines to be detected at night on the surface. An equally significant development was the transfer, in April 1941, of the operational control of RAF Coastal Command to the Admiralty so that better use could be made of the available aircraft, although most long-range aircraft which could have extended the reach of air cover were still being allocated to Bomber Command. Finally, the convoy system was gradually extended westwards, initially from 20°W to 30°W, and then to 35°W, while Canadian and US escort groups began to provide cover in the western Atlantic. By June 1941, convoys had a continuous escort for the whole voyage although there was still an immense area in mid-Atlantic where no air cover was available.

THE U-BOATS PREVAIL: Paradoxically, the progress made in the battle against the U-boats received a major setback with the entry of the United States into the war against Germany following the Japanese attack on Pearl Harbor on 7 December 1941. Previously restrained from operating in the western Atlantic to avoid provoking American reaction, the U-boats were now free to range right up to the American East Coast and into the Caribbean, areas where the US Navy was totally unprepared. For the next six months the German U-boats ranged off the American coast, where the pickings were much easier than fighting against the well-drilled convoys on the British side of the Atlantic. In such circumstances the U-boats took a dreadful toll and, indeed, the U-boat crews referred to it as their 'happy time'. In January 1942 alone, a total of fifty-eight Allied merchant vessels were lost in the North Atlantic and only three of these were from escorted convoys, most of the remainder being off the US East Coast.

As the US Navy gradually organised its coastal defences, the U-boats moved south into the Caribbean and the approaches to the Panama Canal, where they continued to exact a sickening toll. Eventually, by the institution of convoys, construction and provision of more escort craft, and the establishment of air patrols, the level of merchant ship losses was brought down to manageable proportions and the U-boats were forced to retreat to more distant waters. Nevertheless, the figures for 1942 made depressing reading, with total Allied losses reaching 1,664 ships of some 7.8 million tons, of which 1,160 (6.3 million tons) was accounted for by U-boats. Some ninety-two U-boats were sunk in the twelve months from December 1941 and, again, the majority were towards the end of the year as countermeasures grew more effective.

THE CRISIS: The early months of 1943 turned out to be the most critical of the whole battle and, initially, it looked as if the U-boats were still winning. In February they sank 108 ships and a similar number the following month for the loss of only fifteen U-boats while at that time there was a daily average of 116 on patrol in the North Atlantic. Britain had only three months' supply of food stocks and even these could not be maintained if losses continued to escalate, despite the fact that the building of new merchant ships was just beginning to exceed the rate of loss for the first time. Nevertheless, unless a miracle occurred, there was a very real chance that Britain could be starved into submission and certainly there was no prospect of ever transporting enough men and material to allow an assault on Hitler's Europe.

And yet, a miracle did occur and the situation was changed virtually overnight early in May 1943. In particular, the epic crossing of eastbound convoy ONS5 illustrated the change that was occurring in a most emphatic manner. In atrocious weather conditions, some fifty-one U-boats were deployed against the convoy of forty-two merchant ships escorted by a maximum of nine escorts under Commander P.W. Gretton RN. Thirteen merchant ships were indeed sunk but, given the scale of the attack, it could have been much worse. However, the surface escorts sank five U-boats and Catalina flying boats got another pair. This was a major turnaround in Allied fortunes, for only two months earlier, thirty-eight U-boats had attacked two convoys totalling ninety-two ships and had sunk twenty-two for the loss of only one of their own. The new Allied successes in May were backed up with a major campaign by RAF Coastal Command against U-boats transiting across the Bay of Biscay from their base ports to the North Atlantic. The advent of new aircraft equipped with radar and the Leigh Light, a device to illuminate submarines on the surface at night, meant that a heavy toll was taken. In May alone, a total of thirty-eight U-boats were lost from all causes and only twenty-six replacements were completed in that time.

It was a combination of several factors that led to the Allied successes. One of the most significant was the increasing availability of very long-range patrol aircraft such as the four-engined Liberator, which finally closed the mid-Atlantic gap and allowed convoys to receive continuous air support for the whole crossing. The patrol aircraft were backed up by aircraft embarked on the new breed of escort carriers, some of which were organised into hunting groups and achieved some spectacular results from 1943 onwards. As well as improved air cover, the convoys were now accompanied by stronger escort groups comprising more modern and better armed ships. New sonars were developed which could pinpoint and hold a submerged U-boat as the escort manoeuvred for a kill, this being achieved by new weapons such as Hedgehog and Squid which could fire projectiles and depth charges several hundred yards ahead of the attacking ship before the U-boat could take evasive action. Ships were equipped with new radars and radio direction-finding gear which could locate and pinpoint surfaced U-boats long before they could get close to a convoy. To use the new weapons, ships and aircraft to maximum effectiveness, a new science of operational analysis was invented.

THE CLOSING STAGES: By the end of May 1943, Admiral Doenitz had accepted defeat and withdrew the U-boats from the North Atlantic, an action that had a dramatic effect on Allied merchant ships losses, which actually sank to zero in that area between June and August. However, the battle was not over, especially as Germany actually produced more U-boats in 1943 and 1944 than in any other of the war years. In addition they introduced numerous technical advances in an attempt to regain the initiative. One of these was the use of a Schnorkel, which enabled a submarine to run on its diesel engines and charge its batteries while submerged at periscope depth. Another was the GNAT, an electrically powered torpedo which utilised acoustic homing and was specifically intended to attack and sink escort vessels. Initially it achieved some success until the Allies developed an acoustic towed decoy known as Foxer. While the great majority of the wartime U-boats utilised conventional diesel/electric propulsion, the Walter closed-cycle system was installed in the small 300-ton Type XVII U-boat, which was capable of over 20 knots submerged for ranges in excess of 100 miles. These were built in small numbers but had little operational success. A more significant development was the 1,600-ton Type XXI which, although conventionally powered, had a streamlined hull and much increased battery capacity to achieve 16 knots submerged. Equipped with new active and passive sonar systems, these boats posed a significant threat and were a potential war-winning weapon. Fortunately for the Allies, they came too late to affect the outcome.

Following the setbacks in mid-1943, U-boat operations dispersed to other areas, although there were occasional forays into the North Atlantic which met with little success. With the introduction of the Schnorkel, large numbers of U-boats were deployed in British coastal waters, where conditions were more difficult for anti-submarine warfare, and they posed a significant problem for the rest of the war, necessitating the deployment of large numbers of escorts and aircraft to counter them. However, the U-boats were unable to affect the outcome of the Allied invasion of Normandy in June 1944 and over a dozen were sunk while attempting to attack the troop transports. With the capture of the French ports by the Allies, U-boat operations were restricted to Norwegian ports.

One of the outstanding features of the U-boat war was the manner in which morale of their crews never faltered, despite the staggeringly high losses experienced, right up to the German surrender on 8 May 1945. During the whole war, a total of 781 U-boats (out of 1,162 completed) were lost to all causes, taking with them over 32,000 officers and men. On the other side of the balance sheet, they had sunk 14.5 million tons of Allied shipping, involving the loss of around 45,000 lives from the crews of Allied naval and merchant vessels. In May 1945, a total of 159 U-boats surrendered in accordance with the agreed terms while over 200 more were scuttled.

THE IMPORTANCE OF ULTRA: As is now well known, British cryptographers had succeeded in breaking the codes used by the German Enigma machine. The resulting intelligence made available to Allied commanders was referred to as Ultra, and the use of such data was co-ordinated by the Admiralty to assist in the fight against the U-boats. The Naval Intelligence Division also relied on other sources such as direction finding and traffic analysis to build up a reasonably accurate picture of U-boat dispositions. By mid-1941, Ultra was providing really solid information which enabled many convoys to be successfully rerouted to avoid U-boat concentrations. However, this advantage was lost in February 1942 when the Germans added an extra wheel to the Enigma machine. The situation was compounded by the fact that around that time the German B-Dienst (*Beobachtungsdienst*, observation service) achieved a breakthrough in reading Allied naval codes. For the rest of the year the advantage lay with the Germans and it was not until December that the new 'Shark' code was finally broken and high-grade Ultra information started to flow again. It was only just in time, as the U-boat onslaught in early 1943 was the most relentless of the war but, as already related, the turning point was approaching and the use of Ultra was a vital factor in the eventual Allied victory.

Many older destroyers were modified to act as escorts. This is HMS Whitehall, *a V&W class destroyer modified as a long-range escort by the removal of the forward boiler room, fore funnel, all torpedo tubes and two 4.7in guns. This made room for a Hedgehog mortar on the forecastle and additional depth charge racks and mortars aft. Note the tall mainmast carrying the antenna for HF/DF equipment. (NARA)*

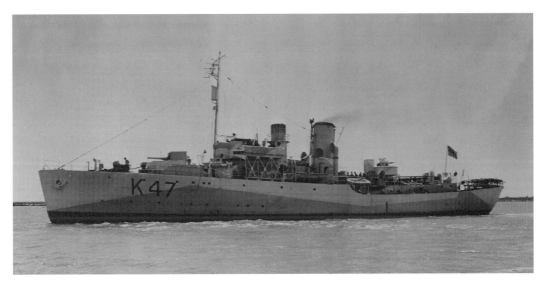

Originally intended as escorts for coastal convoys, the Flower class corvettes became the mainstay of Atlantic convoy escort forces in the early years of the war and a total of 294 were built in British and Canadian yards. This is HMS Polyanthus, *which commissioned in April 1941. A notable feature is the 'lantern' housing for the Type 271 radar mounted at the after end of the bridge. (NARA)*

The U-boats spent much of their patrols on the surface, where they were vulnerable to air attack. Here lookouts aboard U-86 watch for aircraft while also scanning the horizon for possible targets. (NARA)

A merchant ship lies abandoned and on fire after being torpedoed by a U-boat. (NARA)

In late 1940, after losses in Norway and at Dunkirk, the Royal Navy was desperately short of destroyers and virtually none were available to assist with escorting convoys. In the circumstances the transfer of fifty old US Navy destroyers to the Royal Navy was most welcome. Named after towns common to the UK and US, a few were subsequently transferred to the Royal Canadian Navy, including HMCS Hamilton *shown here.* (NARA)

Originally known as twin-screw corvettes, the River class frigates began to enter service from mid-1942 onwards and were larger and better armed than the Flower class corvettes. This is HMS Helford, *which was laid down on 27 June 1942 and commissioned almost exactly a year later, on 26 June 1943.* (NARA)

Above: *Captain Frederick Walker, bareheaded at the front of the bridge of HMS* Starling, *was one of the foremost exponents of anti-submarine warfare. In total, ships of the escort groups that he commanded sank at least seventeen U-boats before his premature death, brought on by stress and overwork, in July 1944.* (AC)

Opposite above: *Until mid-1943, the Short Sunderland flying boat was the only long-range patrol aircraft available to RAF Coastal Command but even so, it lacked the range to completely cover the mid-Atlantic gap between areas patrolled by shore-based aircraft. It was not until the introduction of the PB4Y Liberator that the gap was closed in mid-1943.* (NARA)

Opposite below: *Also from mid-1943, air cover became available from aircraft based on the new breed of escort carriers which entered service in significant numbers in that year. This is HMS* Biter, *one of the first of thirty-eight US-built escort carriers delivered to the Royal Navy under Lend-Lease agreements.* (NARA)

Above: *Taking over from Admiral Sir Percy Noble as Commander-in-Chief Western Approaches in November 1942, Admiral Sir Max Horton presided over the eventual defeat of the U-boat. Here, he is tasting the fruits of victory as he boards a surrendered Type IXC40 U-boat (*U-532*) at Liverpool in June 1945.* (NARA)

Below: (ASM)

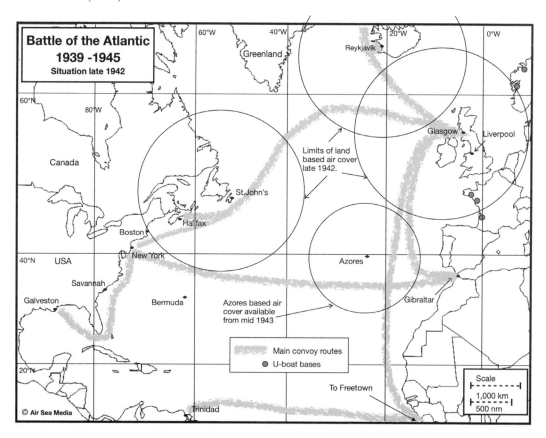

Part Two
The Mediterranean Sea

After the Italian entry into the war in July 1940, the Royal Navy more than held its own and gained an early ascendency in the Action off Calabria, a brief engagement which involved the entire British Mediterranean Fleet and a substantial Italian force. The latter broke off the action when the *Warspite* scored a hit on the Italian battleship *Giulio Cesare* at the staggering range of 26,000 yards. The Royal Navy subsequently reduced the Italian numerical superiority in a night attack by carrier-based aircraft on the defended harbour at Taranto. For propaganda reasons, during the Second World War the Italian Navy was portrayed as being timid and reluctant to fight. However, this was not a true picture and many Italian ships fought bravely while frogman attacks on the British fleet at Alexandria rank among the most daring of the war. The Italian Navy fought at a considerable disadvantage as they had little or no training or equipment for night actions and for most of the period under review they did not possess radar.

Much of the naval action in the Mediterranean was inextricably bound up with the various land campaigns, especially the ongoing pendulum of advance and retreat in the Western Desert. The transport of troops to Greece triggered a major naval action off Cape Matapan in which three Italian cruisers were sunk. British troops then had to be evacuated from Greece and, later, from Crete. These operations cost the Royal Navy dear in the early part of 1941, with several cruisers and destroyers lost to fierce air attack. In North Africa the famous Afrika Korps, with their inspirational leader Erwin Rommel, lost no time in pushing the British back, but as they did so their need for reinforcements and supplies constantly increased and the island of Malta began to assume major strategic importance as it straddled the various sea routes to Libya. British submarines, surface ships and aircraft began to take an unacceptable toll and this provoked a reaction in which Axis air power attempted to isolate and reduce the island by air attack. Running supply convoys from Alexandria became almost impossible due to the German air forces in Libya and Crete so, in July 1941, the first major relief convoy from Gibraltar was organised and another convoy in September (Operation Halberd) was also successful, but thereafter the situation became critical.

In November 1941 the carrier *Ark Royal* was torpedoed and sunk by a U-boat, and a similar fate befell the battleship *Barham* the same month. In December, the Malta-based Force K was almost destroyed by mines but an even worse disaster occurred at Alexandria, where Italian frogmen using human torpedoes succeeded in severely damaging the battleships *Queen Elizabeth* and *Valiant*. By the start of 1942, the Royal Navy in the Mediterranean was in eclipse and in North Africa Rommel was able to take the offensive. At the end of June he had advanced deep into Egypt and was threatening Alexandria. At the same time, Malta was in desperate straits and so an ambitious relief campaign involving convoys from the east and the west was mounted, Operations Harpoon and Vigorous. This was only a marginal success and required a further convoy (Operation Pedestal) in August 1942, which was one of the most ferocious convoy battles of the war. Malta was secured as a result and was able to play its part in Rommel's eventual defeat at El Alamein in November 1942. In the same month, Allied forces had landed in North Africa in Operation Torch, the largest amphibious operation ever mounted up to that time.

By March 1943, Axis forces had been thrown out of North Africa and the era of major naval actions was over. There were, however, several very large-scale amphibious operations to come, each of which would involve substantial naval forces to convey the troops and to provide supply and support after the actual landings. They included Operation Husky, the invasion of Sicily in July 1943, and Operation Avalanche at Salerno in September. This immediately brought about the Italian surrender, although German forces continued the fight. The Italian fleet was ordered to Malta and German air attack sank several ships as they attempted to comply with this instruction. The final major amphibious operation (Dragoon) in the Mediterranean was in August 1944, when Allied troops went ashore in the South of France.

Mers-el-Kébir – Oran (Operation Catapult)

Date:	3 July 1940
Location:	Mers–el–Kébir harbour, western Algeria

British Forces

Commander:	Vice Admiral Sir James Somerville RN (Flag Officer, Force H)
Ships:	Aircraft carrier: *Ark Royal*. Battlecruiser: *Hood*. Battleships: *Resolution, Valiant*. Light cruisers: *Arethusa, Enterprise*. Destroyers: *Faulknor, Fearless, Foxhound, Forester, Foresight, Escort, Keppel, Active, Wrestler, Vortigern, Vidette*

French Forces

Commander:	Admiral Marcel-Bruno Gensoul
Ships:	Battleships: *Dunkerque, Strasbourg, Provence, Bretagne*. Large destroyers: *Mogador, Volta, Tigre, Lynx, Kersaint, Le Terrible*. Seaplane tender: *Commandant Teste*

BACKGROUND: The defeat of France in May and June 1940 posed a potentially serious problem for the British. If there was the slightest chance that Germany would be able to take over French ships under Vichy control then the whole balance of maritime power would be altered. Churchill acted almost immediately and ordered a powerful naval force to Gibraltar, where it had assembled by 30 June. Including the aircraft carrier *Ark Royal*, battlecruiser *Hood*, and battleships *Resolution* and *Valiant*, Force H was commanded by Vice Admiral James Somerville. Its immediate task was, on Churchill's direct orders, to attempt to persuade the French ships in the Algerian ports of Oran and Mers-el-Kébir to join the Allied cause. If not then other courses of action were offered to the French in the hope that they would at least put their ships out of reach of the Germans. The options were set out in a formal document to be delivered to the French naval commander,

Admiral Gensoul, and Somerville was ordered to make it clear that he had orders to sink and destroy the French ships if they would not accept any of the alternatives.

THE ACTION: Force H sailed from Gibraltar on the evening of 2 July and by dawn the following day the ships lay hull down off the port of Oran and the anchorage of Mers-el-Kébir, a little to the west of the main port. The destroyer *Foxhound* was sent ahead carrying Somerville's emissary, Captain Cedric Holland. However, Admiral Gensoul refused to meet him and the written version, including the ultimatum of force, was delivered to the admiral by a junior French officer. In these circumstances, Gensoul's reaction was predictable. He refused point-blank to consider any of the alternatives offered, but stated categorically that the French Navy would never allow any of its ships to be taken over by the Germans, being prepared to scuttle and destroy them if necessary. Eventually, Gensoul agreed to meet Holland and this raised hopes that a compromise could be reached. The meeting was cordial but strained and came to a close when Holland was shown a message just received from the French C-in-C, Admiral Darlan. This effectively ordered Gensoul to resist any attempts to capture or destroy his ships and also ordered other French naval and air forces to act in support. It was obvious that a final showdown was near and Holland left the *Dunkerque* at 1725, only five minutes before an ultimatum issued by Somerville would expire. In fact, the British admiral further delayed the final order, but by then he was being put under considerable pressure by messages from Churchill demanding to know what was happening. In addition, any further delay would give the French ships cover of darkness to escape. With a heavy heart, the order to open fire was given at 1754.

The main targets were the four French battleships moored stern on to the long breakwater mole that stretched to the south-east from the headland on which was sited Fort Mers-el-Kébir. The British ships were to the north-west and their plunging fire came over the headland into the harbour. During the hours of negotiations the French had plenty of time to raise steam and prepare themselves as much as possible for action. Thus, when the British opened fire, Gensoul immediately ordered them to get under way. The destroyers anchored in the roads were to precede the battleships and they quickly moved out, initially unaffected by the British gunfire that was directed at the battleships. Although the first salvo fell short, the remainder was appallingly accurate and caused immense damage and destruction. The *Dunkerque* was hit by several 15in shells just as she was beginning to gather way. With her steering gear wrecked and numerous fires breaking out, she drifted out into mid-channel before temporary repairs brought her under control and her main armament fired several salvoes at the *Hood* in reply, although she was subsequently beached on the western shore.

Of the older battleships, *Bretagne* was hit almost immediately and with fierce fires raging she rolled over and sank within ten minutes, taking over 800 of her crew with her. The *Provence* did succeed in getting under way and opened fire before a hit on the stern caused serious damage and effectively put her out of action, although she remained afloat and was eventually beached. The remaining modern battleship, *Strasbourg*, was more fortunate. She succeeded in making a prompt getaway from the jetty, shells falling into her vacant berth literally seconds after she had got under way, and was able to set off down the main channel towards the open Mediterranean. Ahead of her, the six destroyers were forming up in line ahead and were already clearing harbour when the leading ship, *Mogador*, was hit. Exploding depth charges blew off her stern and she slewed to a halt, later to be taken in tow and beached. The others were undamaged and, with the *Strasbourg* following magnificently astern, headed out to the east.

The British bombardment lasted only ten minutes and fire was halted when the heavy pall of smoke from the sinking and damaged ships obscured all targets, including the escaping *Strasbourg*. Somerville then ordered his ships to steer to the west, convinced that he had achieved his objective, and he did not want further unnecessary loss of life. In addition, as his aircraft had previously mined the harbour entrance, he thought that no ship would be able to escape unscathed. In fact, none of the escaping French ships were affected by the mines and it was not until a Swordfish aircraft reported at 1818 that the *Strasbourg* was away from the harbour that he realised the true situation. By this time the two forces were steering in opposite directions and although the *Hood* turned in pursuit, the only possible way of hitting at the *Strasbourg* was by *Ark Royal*'s aircraft. Six Swordfish armed with bombs had just taken off for a strike against the harbour and these were diverted to chase after the French battleship. They delivered their attack at 1845, just as night was falling, but by this time the *Strasbourg* had been joined by other destroyers sailing from the port of Oran and together they put up concentrated AA fire which resulted in the loss of two aircraft. The *Strasbourg* was undamaged.

The last attempt to halt the *Strasbourg* occurred at 2055, when six torpedo-armed Swordfish made a well-co-ordinated night attack against the fleeing battleship. Although one hit was claimed, she did not slow down and eventually made Toulon in the evening of 4 July to a rapturous reception. Prior to that, Somerville had broken off the pursuit at 2200 on the evening of the 3rd and had altered course back to the west, eventually reaching Gibraltar also on the evening of the 4th. However, the task was not quite complete. Aerial reconnaissance, supported by French communiqués, indicated that the *Dunkerque* was not as badly damaged as was first thought and still posed a possible threat. Somerville was therefore ordered to return and finish her off, although this was to be done by an air strike alone. The attack was duly carried out on 6 July by Swordfish from *Ark Royal* and the battleship was completely disabled.

The *Dunkerque* was eventually made seaworthy enough to return to Toulon, along with the damaged *Provence*. However, both of these ships, and the *Strasbourg*, were scuttled along with the other ships of the French fleet in November 1942 when the Germans occupied Vichy France. This was exactly what the French had promised would happen and served to illustrate that perhaps the action at Mers-el-Kébir had been unnecessary. Churchill had not been prepared to take that chance and the action had at least demonstrated to the world at large that Britain was not defeated and was determined to fight to the last. Total French casualties were 1,147 dead and the memories of Oran soured Anglo–French relations for many years afterwards.

Above: *The destroyer HMS* Foxhound *carried the British emissary, Captain Holland, for negotiations with the French commander, Admiral Gensoul.* (ASM)

Opposite: *Admiral Somerville (right) had the dreadful responsibility of ordering the Royal Navy ships to open fire on their erstwhile French allies. Here he paces the deck of the carrier* Ark Royal *with her commanding officer, Captain Holland (left).* (NARA)

The French battlecruiser Strasbourg *with her sister ship,* Dunkerque, *in the background pictured in happier times. In 1940 these two ships were amongst the most modern and powerful units of the French Navy.* (NARA)

The 15in guns of the R class battleship HMS Resolution, *along with those of HMS* Valiant *and the battlecruiser HMS* Hood, *were responsible for the destruction wrought at Oran on 3 July 1940.* (NARA)

The battleship Bretagne *on fire, down by the stern, and slowly sinking. Behind her is the seaplane tender* Commandant Teste, *which was undamaged and subsequently rescued many survivors from the sunken battleship.* (AC)

The super destroyer Volta *was one of five destroyers that escaped from Mers–el-Kébir and safely made it back to Toulon in company with the* Strasbourg. (NARA)

A view of the Dunkerque *beached after the bombardment and subsequently further damaged by a torpedo from a Swordfish. Following temporary repairs she was finally able to sail for Toulon, which she reached on 20 February 1941.* (AC)

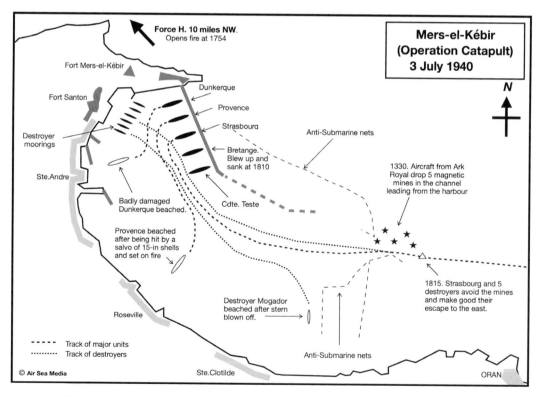

(ASM)

Sinking of the *Bartolomeo Colleoni*

Date:	19 July 1940
Location:	Off Cape Spada, Crete

Allied Forces

Commander:	Force A: Commander Hugh St Lawrence Nicolson.
	Force B, Captain John Augustine Collins RAN
Ships:	Force A: Destroyers: *Hyperion*, *Hero*, *Hasty*, *Ilex*.
	Force B, Cruiser: *Sydney*. Destroyer: *Havock*

Italian Forces

Commander:	Vice Admiral Ferdinando Casardi
Ships:	Cruisers: *Bartolomeo Colleoni*, *Giovanni delle Bande Nere*

BACKGROUND: On 11 June 1940, Italy entered the war as an Axis partner with Germany. With the fall of France on 22 June, the strategic situation in the Mediterranean was precarious from the British point of view and although the possibility of the French ships being taken over by Germany was reduced by the actions at Oran, there was still a sizeable Italian fleet. However, the C-in-C Mediterranean, Admiral Sir A.B. Cunningham, immediately adopted an offensive stance which initially resulted in the indecisive action off Calabria on 8/9 July. He followed this up with the deployment of the 2nd Destroyer Flotilla (designated Force A) to the Aegean Sea for an anti-submarine sweep as a prelude to troop convoys passing through that area carrying reinforcements to Greece. Force A would be supported by the Australian light cruiser HMAS *Sydney* and an escorting destroyer, HMS *Havock*. By coincidence the Italian Navy had planned to send two cruisers (*Bande Nere*, *Bartolomeo Colleoni*) into the Aegean to disrupt British shipping movements. Leaving Tripoli on the evening of 17 July, by dawn on the 19th they were entering the Aegean through the Antikithera Channel a few miles WNW of Cape Spada on the north-west tip of Crete.

THE ACTION: At 0722 on the morning of the 19th, the two Italian cruisers were spotted by the destroyers of Force A, at which point Vice Admiral Casardi, assuming that they were screening a heavier force, turned onto a northerly course. Commander Nicolson brought his destroyers around to a north-easterly course to open the range as the Italian cruisers opened fire and also to lead them towards HMAS *Sydney*, which was now approaching from the north. The Italian ships turned to run parallel to the British destroyers but fortunately, against the fast-moving destroyers, the Italian gunnery was not very accurate and no damage was done. Suddenly, at 0830, the Italian cruisers turned away and headed south-west and then south-east as they had spotted the *Sydney* approaching rapidly from the north. The Australian cruiser had opened fire at a range of 20,000 yards and the arriving salvoes took the Italians completely by surprise.

The action now developed into a long-range stern chase with *Sydney*, now accompanied by five destroyers, in pursuit. The Italian cruisers started laying smoke, which caused Sydney to shift target several times, although an early hit was scored on the *Bande Nere* with no significant damage being done. *Sydney* received a single hit from a 6in shell at 0921, but by that time it was clear that the *Colleoni* was in trouble as she was slowing down and by 0923 was lying stopped only 5 miles ENE of Cape Spada. Leaving the destroyers to finish off the crippled cruiser with torpedoes (she finally sank at 0959), Captain Collins continued in pursuit of the *Bande Nere*. However, the range remained at 20,000 yards and then slowly increased. At that point *Sydney* had expended virtually all the ammunition for her forward turrets (which were the only ones that could bear) and reluctantly Collins gave up the chase at 1037, recalling the destroyers *Hero* and *Hasty*, which had also been unable to get close enough for a torpedo attack. The other destroyers had stayed with the *Colleoni* and between them picked up 525 survivors out of a crew of 630 (another seven were subsequently picked up over the next two days).

On paper the Italian cruisers should easily have been able to outstrip the *Sydney*, which at best was only capable of 32 knots whereas the Italian ships were supposed to be to be able to make at least 34 knots even in loaded condition. The main factor in the outcome was the magnificent gunnery of HMAS *Sydney*, which achieved outstanding results under the conditions of extreme range and high-speed manoeuvring. This was in stark contrast to the Italian gunnery, which was erratic and only scored a single hit. This spirited action was a further morale boost to the Royal Navy's Mediterranean Fleet. As a footnote, although the *Bande Nere* escaped on this occasion, she was torpedoed and sunk by HM Submarine *Urge* on 1 April 1942.

The cruiser HMAS Sydney *was one of three Apollo class light cruisers originally built for the Royal Navy but transferred to Australia before the war.* (SVL)

Action photo showing the Bartolomeo Colleoni *surrounded by shell splashes from the British ships.* (SVL)

With fires raging and her bow blown off by a torpedo, the Colleoni *is slowly sinking.* (SVL)

The Colleoni's *sister ship,* Giovanni delle Bande Nere, *was slightly damaged in the action off Cape Spada but was able to outpace her pursuers and make good her escape.* (NHIC)

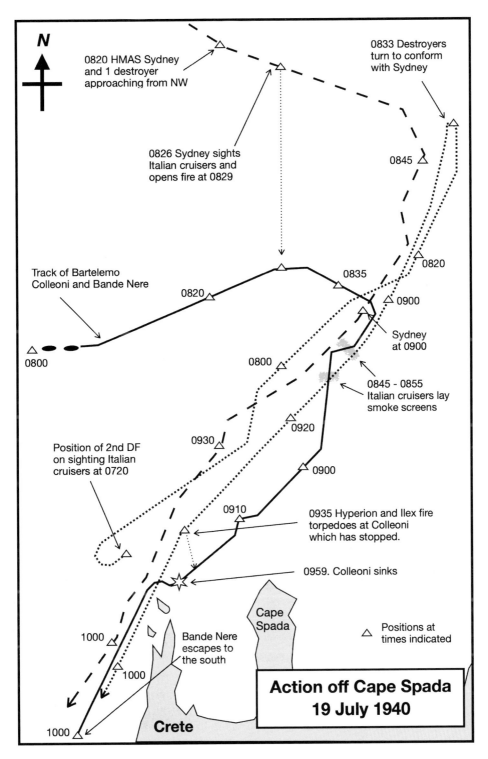

Action off Cape Spada
19 July 1940

(ASM)

Taranto (Operation Judgement)

Date:	11 November 1940
Location:	Taranto harbour, southern Italy

Allied Forces

Commanders:	Admiral Sir Andrew Browne Cunningham RN (C-in-C Mediterranean Fleet), Rear Admiral Arthur Lumley St George Lyster RN (Rear Admiral, Aircraft Carriers)
Ships:	Aircraft carrier: *Illustrious*. Cruisers: *Gloucester*, *Glasgow*, *Berwick*, *York*. Four destroyers

Axis Forces

Commanders:	Admiral Inigo Campioni (C-in-C, Italian fleet), Admiral Arturo Riccardi (Admiral Commanding Taranto)
Ships:	Battleships: *Vittorio Veneto, Littorio, Conte di Cavour, Giulio Cesare, Andrea Doria, Caio Duilio*. Cruisers: *Pola, Zara, Fiume, Gorizia, Trento, Trieste, Bolzano, Giuseppe Garibaldi, Abruzzi*. Twenty-eight destroyers and other additional vessels

BACKGROUND: After Oran, the balance of naval power in the Mediterranean still lay clearly with the Italian fleet. Their battleships, comprising two modern Littorio class and four older but extensively modernised Cavour/Doria classes, were a serious threat. However, the Royal Navy did have the advantage of aircraft carriers and two, *Illustrious* and *Eagle*, were assigned to Admiral Cunningham. The attack on Taranto by aircraft from both carriers, codenamed Operation Judgement, was initially planned for 21 October, the anniversary of the Battle of Trafalgar, but was postponed at the last minute and it was not until early November that another opportunity occurred. On 11 November, having safely escorted a convoy to Malta and reinforced by two additional battleships, Cunningham manoeuvred some 300 miles south of Taranto awaiting the onset of darkness before detaching *Illustrious*, and her escort of four cruisers and four destroyers, north to the planned flying-off position, some 170 miles south-east of Taranto.

THE ACTION: The original plan to launch a combined strike of thirty Swordfish aircraft from the carriers *Illustrious* and *Eagle* had received a setback when the latter had problems with her petrol supply system due to damage caused by earlier bombing attacks. Six of her aircraft were therefore transferred to *Illustrious*, although only a total of twenty-one were eventually available for the operation. They were launched in two waves, the first at 2020 consisting of twelve Swordfish, and the second, an hour later, should have comprised nine aircraft. However, a flight deck accident prevented one from taking off and a technical problem forced another to return. Eventually the damaged aircraft was repaired and it took off twenty-five minutes after the others.

The port at Taranto consisted of an inner landlocked harbour (Mare Piccolo) and an outer anchorage (Mare Grande) protected by breakwaters. The main targets were the two Littorio class and three Cavour class battleships anchored in the Mare Grande, which were protected by torpedo nets and barrage balloons as well as by substantial shore-based AA batteries. As the first wave approached overhead the defences were already alerted and opened fire. Two aircraft overflew the harbour, dropping flares to illuminate the scene before carrying out dive-bombing attacks. Three more Swordfish came in very low from the west and launched torpedoes at the *Conte di Cavour*, scoring one hit. Another two Swordfish attacked the *Littorio* and both torpedoes hit, but a third aircraft was not so successful. The remaining aircraft dropped bombs on the seaplane base adjacent to the dockyard and also damaged a destroyer. Despite the vicious AA fire and the dangers presented by the barrage balloon wires, only the one aircraft was lost and the survivors headed back to the *Illustrious*, landing on from around 0120.

The attack by the second wave followed a similar profile although by now the defences were thoroughly alerted and put up a tremendous barrage as the Swordfish approached. Two aircraft dropped flares before bombing the oil storage depot, leaving the five torpedo-armed aircraft to go in at low level. These obtained another hit on the *Littorio* and also struck the *Caio Duilio*. One aircraft was lost in this attack, but the others successfully evaded the defences and returned safely. The final attack of the evening was by the late straggler from the second flight, which arrived well after the others and made a leisurely bombing attack on two cruisers, scoring a hit on the *Trento* although the bomb failed to explode. This last aircraft of the second strike landed on *Illustrious* at 0255 and the carrier then turned south to rejoin the main fleet and to escape the retaliatory air attacks which could be expected the next day. In fact, these did not transpire and all ships arrived safely back at Alexandria on 14 November.

Subsequent reports determined that the *Littorio* had been hit by three torpedoes and, while she did not sink, the damage was serious and she was out of action for five months. The *Caio Duilio* was hit by a single torpedo on the starboard side, which resulted in severe flooding and the ship was beached in order to prevent her sinking. She was not fully repaired until the following May. The most seriously damaged was the *Conte di Cavour*, which although only hit by a single torpedo nevertheless settled on the bottom with her upper deck submerged. She was eventually refloated in July 1941, but saw no further service. In all, this was an outstanding success by a relatively small number of aircraft and it materially altered the balance of power in the Mediterranean.

Above: *The attack on Taranto was launched from the carrier HMS* Illustrious, *which joined the Mediterranean Fleet at the end of August 1940.* (ASM)

Opposite above: *Fairey Swordfish ranged on deck and being prepared for action. Obsolete even at the start of the war, this venerable biplane contributed to many successful actions, not least the valiant attack on the Italian fleet at Taranto.* (NARA)

Opposite below: *The Italian battleship* Conte di Cavour *was initially completed in 1915 but in the 1930s was substantially rebuilt and modernised. Hit by a single torpedo in the Taranto attack, she nevertheless sank in shallow water with her decks awash and was never returned to service.* (NHIC)

The modern battleship Littorio *had only commissioned in May 1940 but was hit by three torpedoes during the attack. In this subsequent aerial photo she is surrounded by tugs and salvage vessels, and the bow is underwater.* (NHIC)

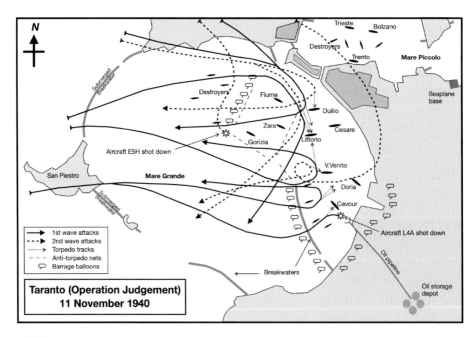

(ASM)

Battle of Matapan

Date:	28 March 1941
Location:	Approximately 100 miles west of Crete

Allied Forces

Commanders:	Force A: Admiral Sir Andrew Browne Cunningham RN (C-in-C Mediterranean Fleet), Force B: Vice Admiral Henry Daniel Pridham-Wippel (Vice Admiral Light Forces)
Ships:	Force A: Aircraft carrier *Formidable*. Battleships: *Warspite, Valiant, Barham*. Destroyers: *Jervis, Janus, Mohawk, Nubian* (14th DF), *Stuart, Greyhound, Griffin, Hotspur, Havock* (10th DF)
	Force B: Cruisers: *Orion, Ajax, Perth, Gloucester*. Destroyers: *Ilex, Hasty, Hereward, Vendetta* (2nd DF)

Axis Forces

Commander:	Admiral Angelo Iachino (C-in-C, Italian fleet)
Ships:	Battleship: *Vittorio Veneto*. Cruisers: *Pola, Zara, Fiume* (1st Division); *Trento, Trieste, Bolzano* (3rd Division); *Giuseppe Garibaldi, Abruzzi* (8th Division). Destroyers: *Corazziere, Carabiniere, Ascari, Granatiere, Fucilere, Bersagliere, Alpino, Gioberti, Alfieri, Oriani, Carducci, Da Recco, E. Pessagno*

BACKGROUND: In October 1940, Italian forces invaded Greece. Subsequently, British troops were withdrawn from the Western Desert to reinforce the position in Greece and these were sent in convoys from Alexandria. The lack of Italian success in this theatre, coupled with the build-up of British forces, caused Hitler to demand more positive action from the Italian fleet in advance of his own plans to commit German forces to the area. In response to this prompting, Admiral Iachino planned a powerful sortie against the British convoys in the area west of Crete. On 26 March he sailed from Naples aboard the modern battleship *Vittorio*

Veneto accompanied by four destroyers. His movements were co-ordinated with a force of three heavy cruisers from Taranto, two light cruisers from Brindisi and three more heavy cruisers from Messina, each group accompanied by escorting destroyers. Making rendezvous south of the Strait of Messina on the morning of the 27th, the Italian fleet then set course towards Crete. Later that day an RAF Sunderland flying boat located and reported one of the cruiser divisions some 80 miles east of Sicily, giving Admiral Cunningham his first positive information that the Italians were at sea.

However, the British were already expecting such a move, having been warned by Ultra decodes of the impending operation against the convoys, and the Mediterranean Fleet prepared to sail from Alexandria on the evening of the 27th. In the meantime, a force of four cruisers (*Orion*, *Ajax*, *Perth* and *Gloucester*) and four destroyers under the command of Vice Admiral Pridham-Wippel was ordered from the Aegean Sea to rendezvous with Cunningham at dawn off the island of Gavdos to the south of Crete.

The stage was now set for the largest fleet action to be fought by the Royal Navy in the Second World War. Its battle fleet of one carrier, three battleships, four light cruisers and thirteen destroyers was heading towards the Italian force of one battleship, six heavy and two light cruisers, and thirteen destroyers. Although the British had superiority in battleships, they were all elderly ships of First World War vintage and the fastest (*Valiant*) was only capable of just over 24 knots while the Italian *Vittorio Veneto* was one of the new breed of heavily armoured fast battleships capable of in excess of 30 knots. Also the Italian force included six heavily armed 8in cruisers, against which the smaller British cruisers with their 6in guns were poorly matched. Thus, on paper the fleets were very evenly matched but the British had two priceless advantages of which they made full use. One was an aircraft carrier, although its complement of only twenty-seven aircraft severely limited its offensive capability. The other was radar, which was to prove invaluable, especially in the night actions.

THE ACTION: 28 March turned out to be a busy day for HMS *Formidable*. At 0555 she flew off aircraft to search ahead of the fleet. At 0720, one of these reported sighting four cruisers and four destroyers heading south-west off Gavdos island and, shortly afterwards, a second aircraft reported another sighting of cruisers and destroyers some 20 miles away. These reports were difficult to interpret as it was not clear whether all the ships sighted were Italian or some were in fact Pridham-Wippel's cruisers hurrying to the rendezvous position. This uncertainty was only removed at 0824 when HMS *Orion* reported enemy ships in sight, by which time Pridham-Wippel had ordered his force onto a south-easterly course in order to lead the enemy vessels towards the approaching British battleships. As the faster Italian cruisers (*Trieste*, *Trento*, *Bolzano*) closed the range, they opened fire at 0812, but their gunnery was generally inaccurate and when *Gloucester* started returning fire when within range, they stood off and eventually reversed course to the north-east. The tables were now turned as the Italians attempted to lead the British cruisers back towards the *Vittorio Veneto*, which was now pushing forward at 30 knots in the hope of joining the engagement. Up to this point, neither commanding admiral was aware of the other side's battleships but shortly after 0900, Iachino received a report indicating that the British fleet, consisting of an aircraft carrier and at least two battleships as well as cruisers and destroyers, was approaching from the south. However, he was reluctant to believe the aircraft report and placed greater credence on D/F bearings which put them some 170 miles away.

As Cunningham's battleships continued towards the scene of the action at a stately 22 knots (the best speed of the slowest ship, *Barham*), he ordered a strike by land-based Swordfish from Maleme airfield on Crete and subsequently a strike of six Albacores and two Fulmar fighters was flown off *Formidable* at 0952. An hour later, HMS *Orion*, the leading British cruiser, suddenly sighted the *Vittorio Veneto* at 1058 and although Pridham-Wippel immediately ordered his force to turn back to the south-east, they came under heavy and accurate fire from the battleship and the *Trieste* group of cruisers, which now conformed with their flagship. With Cunningham's battleships still some 80 miles away, the British cruisers were in a critical situation when *Formidable*'s strike force arrived on the scene. Although their attack was pressed home with great determination, they did not score any hits, and three Swordfish of 815 Squadron which arrived shortly afterwards from Crete were also unsuccessful. However, these attacks did prompt Iachino to break off the surface action and alter course to the north-west, his main aim now being to return home and escape further air attack. The British cruisers, no longer threatened, continued their south-easterly course for a while with the intention of joining with Cunningham's main force.

Now that the *Vittorio Veneto* was drawing away, Cunningham ordered another carrier strike to be launched but this again comprised a pitifully small number of aircraft (three Albacores and two Swordfish) and it did not catch up with the Italian battleship until 1519. Nevertheless, they were assisted by the fact that as they manoeuvred to start their attack, a formation of RAF Blenheims was also making a high-level bombing attack. Although such desirable co-ordination was unplanned and entirely accidental, it distracted the attention of the Italian gunners, who were also being subjected to strafing attacks by two of *Formidable*'s Fulmars. Consequently, the low-level torpedo bombers were not spotted until the last minute and were able to drop their torpedoes at close range. The strike leader (Lieutenant Commander J. Dalyell-Stead) released his torpedo but, as he turned away, his aircraft was hacked out of the sky by the now alerted gunners on the *Vittorio Veneto*. Despite this, the torpedo ran true and struck below the stern, damaging the rudders and propellers and bringing the battleship to a temporary halt. Further damage was caused by one of the Blenheim's bombs which scored a very near miss on the stern. As the news reached Cunningham, there was now every prospect that his battleships would be able to catch the damaged Italian battleship and finish her off but, instead, the Italian crew through heroic damage control efforts succeeded in getting their ship under way and eventually she was making off at over 16 knots.

There was no rest for the aircrews aboard *Formidable*, who were now ordered to make a third strike and six Albacores and two Swordfish were launched, these later being reinforced by two more Swordfish from Maleme (Crete). By now Iachino had drawn his cruisers and destroyers around the *Vittorio Veneto* in a protective screen and consequently the air attack beginning at 1925 was met by a wall of AA fire which caused the formations to split up. Although no further hits were obtained on the battleship, one torpedo hit the heavy cruiser *Pola*, which came to a dead stop in the water with her engine rooms flooded. Iachino continued to withdraw but ordered the remaining ships of the 1st Cruiser Division (*Zara* and *Fiume*) together with four destroyers to remain with the damaged cruiser. It was now night and the pursuing British battleships were still relentlessly closing when Admiral Cunningham ordered eight destroyers led by Captain P.J. Mack (D14) ahead in order to catch and attack the *Vittorio Veneto*. In the darkness, neither the destroyers nor Pridham-Wippel's cruisers managed to locate her and she eventually regained the relative safety of Taranto.

In the meantime, Cunningham's battleships were finally joining the battle and, following a report of a radar contact from the cruiser *Achilles*, he was able to bring his ships within range of an unidentified stationary target off the port bow. At almost the same time (2220), one of the British destroyers reported a group of Italian cruisers and destroyers passing in line ahead across the path of the British ships. These were the *Zara* and *Fiume* with their accompanying destroyers sailing to the assistance of their damaged sister ship, totally unaware that they had strayed into the path of the British battle fleet. Cunningham calmly manoeuvred his ships into an ideal firing position on a parallel course using radar information until visual contact was achieved. At 2227, the battleships opened fire on their unsuspecting targets at almost point-blank range. Within minutes, the *Zara* and *Fiume* were blazing wrecks while the destroyers *Griffin*, *Greyhound*, *Stuart* and *Havock* slogged it out with the Italian destroyers, sinking the *Carducci* and finishing off the *Alfieri*, which was already mortally damaged by 15in gunfire from the *Barham*. The other British destroyers which had been sent ahead in the unsuccessful attempt to catch the *Vittorio Veneto* eventually rejoined after 0200 and the flotilla leader, HMS *Jervis*, finished off the *Zara* with torpedoes before going alongside the lifeless *Pola* to take off some 257 survivors. She, in turn, was subsequently sunk by torpedoes from both *Jervis* and *Nubian*.

The destroyers then made off to the east, joining up with the battle fleet at dawn. Although Cunningham brought his ships back to the scene of the action in daylight to search for survivors, he was forced to abandon this humanitarian action and set course for Alexandria when German reconnaissance aircraft appeared. Later in the day, *Formidable* was subjected to a concentrated air attack by Ju 88 dive-bombers but emerged unscathed and the fleet entered Alexandria in the late afternoon on 30 March. It was an outstanding victory for the Mediterranean Fleet under Admiral Cunningham. They had sunk three heavy cruisers and two destroyers for the loss of a single aircraft while *Formidable*'s Fulmars had shot down several Ju 88s attacking the fleet.

The powerful battleship Vittorio Veneto *was the flagship of the Italian fleet at Matapan. Although slowed by a torpedo hit, she was able to escape the slower British battleships which lacked the speed to catch her.* (ASM)

Vice Admiral Pridham-Wippel flew his flag in the light cruiser HMS Orion, which was armed with eight 6in guns. (NARA)

The most powerful cruiser in the British fleet was HMS Gloucester, which carried twelve 6in guns. However, she was still outranged by the heavier 8in guns of the Italian heavy cruisers. (AC)

Fairey Albacores landing aboard HMS Formidable. *These aircraft, flown by 826 and 829 NAS, were responsible for torpedo hits on the* Vittorio Veneto *and the cruiser* Pola. (ASM)

The battleship HMS Valiant *was equipped with a Type 273 radar set, which gave the British fleet a tremendous advantage in the night action.* (NARA)

The Italian heavy cruiser Fiume, *one of three sister ships sunk at Matapan.* (AC)

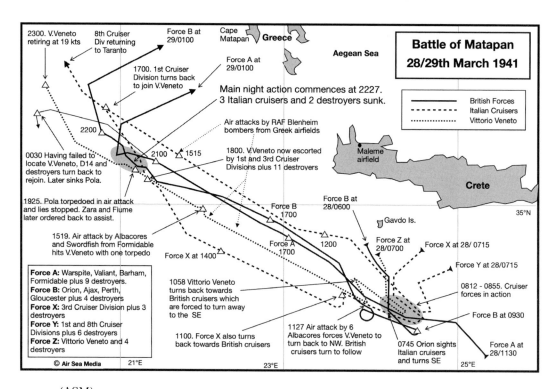

(ASM)

Destruction of the Duisberg Convoy

Date:	9 November 1941
Location:	200 miles east of Malta, central Mediterranean

Allied Forces

Commander:	Captain William Gladstone Agnew RN (Commander Force K)
Ships:	Cruisers: *Aurora, Penelope*. Destroyers: *Lance, Lively*

Axis Forces

Commander:	Vice Admiral Bruno Brivonesi (Commander 3rd Cruiser Division)
Ships:	Cruisers: *Trieste, Trento*. Destroyers: *Alpino, Bersagliere, Fucilere, Granatiere* (13th Destroyer Squadron), *Euro, Fulmine, Grecale, Libeccio, Oriani, Geniere* (convoy escort)

BACKGROUND: By the summer of 1941 the British position the Mediterranean was precarious to say the least. Allied forces had been chased out of Greece and subsequently Crete had fallen to a fierce airborne assault commencing on 20 May. By the end of the month the island was abandoned to the Germans although over 16,000 British and Commonwealth were evacuated to Egypt by the Royal Navy, an operation which cost three cruisers and six destroyers. In North Africa the British Army was on the defensive at the Libya/Egypt Border while the isolated fortress of Tobruk remained under siege from Rommel's forces. Following this there was a stand-off while both sides tried to build up their strength in order to launch an offensive. With Fliegerkorps X based on Sicily, the Luftwaffe controlled the skies over the central Mediterranean (at least by day) and a powerful Italian fleet remained as a potent threat so that British supplies to North Africa were forced to follow the long sea route around the Cape of Good Hope and into the Indian Ocean. Axis supplies faced a much shorter route from Italy across the Mediterranean to Libyan ports and in this situation the British base at Malta was a vital strategic asset. Submarines and aircraft based on the island took a steady toll on Axis shipping and from October

1941 they were supplemented by a number of destroyers and light cruisers which comprised Force K. The arrival of these ships forced the Italians to adopt new routings and tactics and initially they successfully passed two small convoys which Force K failed to intercept. By this time the Royal Navy had access to Ultra intelligence resulting from the breaking of the German Enigma codes and this was backed up by well-organised reconnaissance flights operating out of Malta. From these sources, Captain Agnew, commanding Force K, became aware that a large convoy consisting of six merchant ships escorted by at least four destroyers was already at sea and steering east from Sicily before turning south to pass well east of Malta in order to keep out of range of the island's strike aircraft. However, he did not know that this convoy was supported by a further Italian force consisting of the heavy cruisers *Trento* and *Trieste*, together with two destroyers that had sailed from Messina at noon on 8 October.

THE ACTION: Captain Agnew, flying his flag aboard the cruiser *Aurora*, led Force K out from Valetta harbour at dusk on 8 November and set course to the east. Armed with the Ultra intelligence, his radar-equipped ships eventually located the convoy some 200 miles east of Malta at 0039 on the morning of the 9th. It comprised a total of seven merchant ships, of which the largest included the 7,389grt *Duisberg* and two oil tankers which between them carried approximately 20,000 tons of supplies together with 14,000 tons of oil and petrol. The convoy was arranged in two columns of three ships, *Duisberg* leading the starboard column while the 7,599-ton tanker *Minatitlan* led the port column, and the seventh ship (*Rina Corrado*, 5,180 tons) brought up the rear between the columns. A close escort of six destroyers ringed the convoy while the support force of the heavy cruisers *Trento* and *Trieste* and four more destroyers followed about 2 miles astern. At the time of the sighting, *Aurora* was leading the British line, followed by *Lance*, *Penelope* and *Lively* on a north-easterly course with the convoy now fine on the port bow. Agnew led his ships round onto a northerly course to keep the convoy silhouetted against the moon (and his own ships in darkness), intending to turn in to attack from the convoy's starboard quarter once in a suitable position. Force K had worked together for some time and was now a well-drilled unit with each ship capable of acting on its own initiative in accordance with well-rehearsed tactics.

Lacking radar, the Italians remained oblivious to the approaching threat until, having turned in towards the convoy, *Aurora* opened fire at 0057 with its 6in guns on the nearest destroyer, *Grecale*. At the same time, *Penelope* engaged the *Maestrale* while the British destroyers opened fire on the merchant ships. After several hits on a merchant ship, *Lance* directed her fire onto the destroyer *Fulmine* and a few minutes later, *Penelope* joined in, bringing the Italian destroyer to a standstill in sinking condition. The British force had achieved complete surprise and the Italians were thrown into confusion. Many of the merchant ships thought they were under air attack and started to put up a fierce AA barrage, while hits on the *Maestrale* had carried away her radio aerials so that the commander of the escort force (Captain Ugo Bisciani) could not inform the 3rd Cruiser Division of the situation. Other ships thought that they had mistakenly come under attack from their own cruisers and consequently hesitated to open fire. In the confusion, Agnew led his ships south and then east to pass ahead of the convoy before turning north to pass up the port side of the convoy, which continued to steam steadily on its original course. Despite the efforts of the Italian destroyers to lay smokescreens, the merchant ships were now easy targets and every single one was set ablaze. Lacking unified direction, individual Italian destroyers attempted to engage the British ships, but every one was beaten off in a hail of gunfire. In fact, the standard of British gunnery in this action was exceptionally good, while several torpedo hits were obtained on the merchant ships, hastening their demise.

In the meantime, Admiral Brivonesi, aboard the heavy cruisers, became aware of the situation by means of a signal from the destroyer *Bersagliere* and increased speed to overtake the convoy on its starboard side. Some of the British ships were sighted and *Trieste* commenced firing at a range of over 8,000 yards with no effect. In turn, the Italian ships were sighted from *Aurora* and *Lance* but were mistakenly identified as two merchant ships with escorting destroyers, which Agnew elected to ignore in favour of the main convoy. It was not actually until well after the action that he became aware that the two heavy cruisers had been present. By 0200, Force K had passed around the rear of the convoy and set course for Malta in order to be under fighter cover by dawn, the Italian heavy cruisers having already turned north in an unsuccessful attempt to intercept the British ships as they withdrew. They left behind a scene of chaos and destruction with every one of the seven merchant ships on fire and sinking. In addition, the destroyer *Fulmine* had been sunk, while *Euro*, *Libeccio* and *Grecale* were seriously damaged, the latter taken under tow by *Oriani*. To complete the tally in this astounding action, the damaged *Libeccio* was finished off later the same day by a torpedo from the submarine *Upholder*. In the aftermath the Italian destroyers picked up 693 survivors from the convoy and another sixty-eight were rescued by other vessels.

The ships of Force K were undamaged and suffered not a single casualty – a remarkable result. They returned to a rapturous welcome in Malta and Captain Agnew subsequently received a well-deserved knighthood for his leadership. For the Axis forces in North Africa it was a severe blow, the loss of the vital supplies being keenly felt when the British 8th Army launched a successful offensive only a week later. Force K was very active in various operations to support the land campaign but its run of successes was brought to a sudden and tragic halt on 19 December when the cruiser *Neptune* and destroyer *Kandahar* were lost and *Aurora* was seriously damaged in a German minefield off the Tripoli coast. For several months thereafter the Axis held the upper hand in the central Mediterranean and it was not until the summer of 1942 that the situation at Malta was restored.

HMS Aurora *was one of the two Arethusa class light cruisers which formed part of Force K.* (NARA)

The heavy cruiser Trieste, *together with her sister ship* Trento, *provided the heavy support for the convoy but played little part in the action.* (AC)

The convoy was escorted by no fewer than six destroyers and another four, including the Soldati class Alpino *shown here, accompanied the heavy cruisers.* (WC)

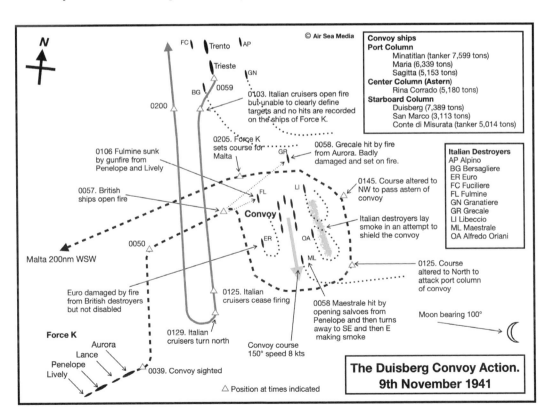

(ASM)

The Battle of Sirte

Date:	22 March 1942
Location:	North of the Gulf of Sirte, eastern Mediterranean

Allied Forces

Commander:	Rear Admiral Sir Philip Louis Vian RN
Ships:	Cruisers: *Cleopatra, Dido, Euryalus, Penelope, Carlisle*. Destroyers: *Jervis, Kingston, Kelvin, Kipling* (14th Flotilla); *Sikh, Zulu, Lively, Hero, Havock, Hasty* (22nd Flotilla); *Legion*. Escort destroyers: *Southwold, Beaufort, Dulverton, Hurworth, Avon Vale, Eridge*

Axis Forces

Commander:	Admiral Angelo Iachino (C-in-C, Italian fleet)
Ships:	Battleship: *Littorio*. Cruisers: *Trento, Gorizia, Bande Nere*. Destroyers: *Ascari, Aviere, Grecale, Oriani, Geniere, Scirocco, Alpino, Bersagliere, Fucilere, Lanciere*

BACKGROUND: From the end of 1941, Malta was increasingly isolated and it became ever more difficult to run supplies through to the island. In December a major naval effort was mounted in order to get a single oil tanker (*Breconshire*) through and this happened to coincide with an attempt by the Italian Navy to run a convoy to Tripoli. This latter was escorted by a strong force including three battleships and two heavy cruisers, which ran into a British force of cruisers and destroyers escorting the *Breconshire* at nightfall on 17 December. Under the command of Rear Admiral Vian, the outnumbered British destroyers and cruisers acted aggressively and the Italian force withdrew under the threat of a night torpedo attack. This skirmish became known as the First Battle of Sirte but was to be followed by a much more complex engagement a few months later when another convoy (MW10) of four fast ships, again including the tanker *Breconshire*, was prepared to sail from Alexandria to Malta. A simultaneous operation by Force H in the western Mediterranean would attempt to fly Spitfires into the beleaguered island. MW10 sailed on 20 March with a close escort consisting of the AA cruiser *Carlisle* and six destroyers (22nd DF) and a covering force of three cruisers and four destroyers (14th DF) with Rear Admiral Vian again in command. The convoy and its escorts were sighted by Italian aircraft and submarines on the following day (21st) and in response Admiral Iachino sailed from Taranto aboard the battleship *Littorio*, accompanied by one light and two heavy cruisers from Messina, as well as several destroyers. On the same day, the convoy's close escort was joined by six Hunt class escort destroyers (5th DF), while on the morning of the 22nd, the covering force was reinforced by the cruiser *Penelope* and destroyer *Legion* from Malta. The stage was set for a major fleet action.

THE ACTION: Vian was aware of the approaching Italian force thanks to Ultra and C38m intercepts but pressed on as planned, enduring a torpedo attack by Italian SM.79 bombers around midday. This was fought off with heavy AA fire but in view of the approaching Italian threat he ordered the 22nd DF to leave the convoy and deploy in support of his cruiser force. For the rest of the day the convoy remained subject to a series of air attacks but was ably defended by the AA fire of the Hunt class destroyers and the AA cruiser *Carlisle*. At 1427, *Euryalus* sighted four enemy ships approaching from the north-east. The convoy and its close escort immediately turned away to the south-west, while Vian's cruisers and destroyers steamed between the fleeing convoy and the approaching Italian cruisers laying a thick smokescreen. There was a strong south-easterly wind, which rapidly spread the smoke but also whipped up the sea, causing the ships of both sides to pitch heavily and making accurate gunnery difficult. Vian's movements caused the Italian ships to break off to the north-west and he therefore led his own ships back towards the convoy, which was now under heavy attack from Luftwaffe Ju 88s. Initially he thought that the Italians had withdrawn but in fact the cruisers had joined up with the *Littorio* and the whole force was sighted again approaching from the north-east at 1640. Vian, flying his flag aboard *Cleopatra*, ordered his cruisers and destroyers out towards the Italian ships. The weather conditions hampered the Italian fire, although *Cleopatra* was struck by a 6in shell and *Euryalus* suffered damage from a 15in shell exploding alongside. However, Iachino was reluctant to approach too close in case he should suffer a torpedo attack from destroyers emerging from the swirling smokescreen. He therefore turned to the west in an attempt to get around the smoke and then attack the convoy.

   This proved to be, literally, a long-winded affair as the smoke was drifting to the north-west and it was not until after 1800 that he eventually turned south and ran down on the convoy. Unfortunately, Vian had anticipated that Iachino might try to pass round to the east of the smokescreen and had stationed some of his cruisers there in anticipation. Thus it fell on the available destroyers to meet the advancing Italians, which they did with great bravery, pressing home to fire torpedoes at ranges of less than 6,000 yards. No hits are scored although both *Havock* and *Kingston* were severely damaged by near misses from 15in shells. Attacks by the Italian destroyers were equally unsuccessful and, with darkness falling, Iachino called off his ships and turned away to the north having achieved nothing despite his overwhelming superiority. In fact, there was worse to come as the destroyers *Lanciere* and *Scirocco* subsequently foundered in the storm, which was increasing in severity through the night.

Meanwhile, Vian ordered the now scattered merchant ships to head independently at their best speed for Malta, each accompanied by a destroyer escort. The freighters *Talabot* and *Pampas* reached Grand Harbour but were then sunk by air attack before their cargo had been unloaded, although some was later salvaged. The *Clan Campbell* was sunk some 20 miles out and the brave *Breconshire* was disabled with only 8 miles to go. Although towed to the south shore along with the damaged destroyer *Legion*, both ships were finished off a few days later. In the end, only some 5,000 tons of supplies was landed out of a total of 26,000 tons aboard the four ships when they had set out from Alexandria. Overall, it was a sad outcome after the brilliance of the cruiser action.

The Dido class light cruiser HMS Cleopatra *was Rear Admiral Vian's flagship during the Second Battle of Sirte.* (ASM)

HMS Carlisle *was a First World War vintage light cruiser which had been converted into an effective anti-aircraft ship by equipping her with high-angle 4in guns and radar. As such she proved her worth when the convoy was subjected to a series of heavy air attacks.* (ASM)

The cruisers HMS Euryalus *(foreground) and HMS* Dido *in company during the battle.* (NARA)

The Italian battleship Littorio *in action. Aggressive tactics and use of smokescreens by the British cruisers and destroyers managed to keep the battleship at bay and she eventually withdrew without causing any damage to the convoy.* (NARA)

A view of the bridge of HMS Euryalus *as she follows astern of HMS* Cleopatra, *which is laying a smokescreen.* (WC)

HMS Jervis *was the leader of the 14th Destroyer Flotilla under Captain A.L. Poland DSO, DSC, which made a spirited torpedo attack on the Italian ships in the closing stages of the action.* (NARA)

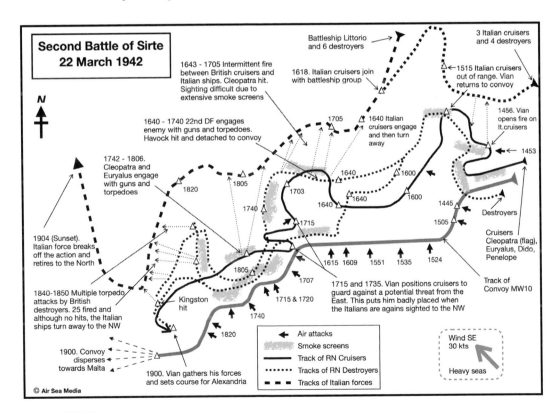

**Second Battle of Sirte
22 March 1942**

N

Battleship Littorio
and 6 destroyers

3 Italian cruisers
and 4 destroyers

1643 - 1705 Intermittent fire
between British cruisers and
Italian ships. Cleopatra hit.
Sighting difficult due to
extensive smoke screens

1618. Italian cruisers join
with battleship group

1515 Italian cruisers
out of range. Vian
returns to convoy

1640 - 1740 22nd DF engages
enemy with guns and torpedoes.
Havock hit and detached to convoy

1705

1640 Italian
cruisers engage
and then turn
away

1456. Vian
opens fire on
It.cruisers

1453

1742 - 1806.
Cleopatra and
Euryalus engage
with guns and
torpedoes

1820

1805

1640

1600

1640

1600

1445

1703

1640

1640

1505

Destroyers

1740

1715

Cruisers
Cleopatra (flag),
Euryalus, Dido,
Penelope

1904 (Sunset).
Italian force breaks
off the action and
retires to the North

1615 1609 1551 1535 1524

Track of
Convoy MW10

1805

1707

1715 and 1735. Vian positions cruisers to
guard against a potential threat from the
East. This puts him badly placed when
the Italians are agains sighted to the NW

1840-1850 Multiple torpedo
attacks by British
destroyers. 25 fired and
although no hits, the Italian
ships turn away to the NW

Kingston
hit

1715 & 1720

1740

1820

Wind SE
30 kts

1900. Convoy
disperses
towards Malta

1900. Vian gathers his forces
and sets course for Alexandria

Heavy seas

← Air attacks

Smoke screens

—— Track of RN Cruisers

········ Tracks of RN Destroyers

■ ■ ■ Tracks of Italian forces

© Air Sea Media

(ASM)

Operations Harpoon and Vigorous

Date:	12 to 16 June 1942
Location:	Eastern and western Mediterranean

Allied Forces (Harpoon)

Commander:	Vice Admiral Alban Thomas Buckley Curteis RN
Ships:	**Force W.** Aircraft carriers: *Eagle*, *Argus*. Battleship: *Malaya*. Cruisers: *Kenya* (flag), *Liverpool*, *Charybdis*, *Welshman*. Destroyers: *Onslow*, *Icarus*, *Escapade*, *Wishart*, *Westcott*, *Wrestler*, *Vidette*, *Antelope*
Ships:	**Force X.** AA Cruiser: *Cairo*. Destroyers: *Bedouin*, *Marne*, *Matchless*, *Ithuriel*, *Partridge*, *Blankney*, *Middelton*, *Badsworth*, *Kujawiak* (Polish Navy). Also four minesweepers and six MGBs

Allied Forces (Vigorous)

Commanders:	Admiral Henry Harwood Harwood RN (C–in–C Mediterranean Fleet), Rear Admiral Sir Philip Louis Vian RN (Commander Escort Force)
Ships:	Cruisers: *Cleopatra*, *Dido*, *Euryalus*, *Hermione*, *Arethusa*, *Coventry* (15th CS), *Birmingham*, *Newcastle* (4th CS). Destroyers: *Fortune*, *Griffin*, *Hotspur* (2nd DD Flotilla), *Dulverton*, *Exmoor*, *Croome*, *Eridge*, *Airedale*, *Beaufort*, *Hurworth*, *Tetcott*, *Aldenham* (5th DD Flotilla), *Napier*, *Nestor*, *Nizam*, *Norman* (7th DD Flotilla), *Jervis*, *Kelvin*, *Javelin* (14th Flotilla); *Pakenham*, *Paladin*, *Inconstant* (12th DD Flotilla); *Sikh*, *Zulu*, *Hasty*, *Hero* (22nd DD Flotilla). Also the demilitarised battleship *Centurion* acting as a decoy

Axis Forces

Commanders:	Admiral Angelo Iachino (C–in–C Italian Fleet). Field Marshal Albert Kesselring (C–in–C German Mediterranean forces)

Ships:	**Eastern Med:** Battleships: *Littorio, Vittorio Veneto.* Cruisers: *Trento, Gorizia* (3rd Division), *Garibaldi, Duca d'Aosta* (8th Division). Destroyers: *Legionario, Folgore, Freccia, Saetta* (7th Flotilla); *Alpino, Bersagliere, Pigafetta, Mitragliere* (13th flotilla); *Aviere, Geniere, Camicia Nera, Corazziere* (11th flotilla). Also six German E-boats
Ships:	**Western Med:** Cruisers: *Eugenio di Savoia, Raimondo Montecuccoli* (7th Division). Destroyers: *Oriani, Ascari, Gioberti*
Submarines:	A total of twenty-seven Italian submarines and German U-boats deployed against both convoys

BACKGROUND: By May 1942, Malta's situation was extremely critical and stocks of food and fuel would be exhausted by the middle of the year. Preparations therefore began for a major convoy operation to take place in mid-June. Five fast freighters were to sail from Gibraltar escorted by a strong surface force including a battleship and two aircraft carriers under the code name Harpoon. Simultaneously, a larger convoy of eleven merchant ships would sail from Alexandria in the east (Operation Vigorous). Although the Mediterranean Fleet at that time had no carriers or battleships, an escort of no less than eight cruisers and twenty-six destroyers was assembled. In addition, some four dozen land-based torpedo aircraft and bombers were available to attack the Italian fleet if it should come out.

OPERATION HARPOON: The western convoy and close escort (Force X, commanded by Captain C.C. Hardy aboard the cruiser *Cairo*) passed Gibraltar on the 12th and was joined by its heavy cover, Force W, later that day. Despite the apparent strength of the escort, the two aircraft carriers were old and small (the newer fleet carriers all being otherwise engaged or refitting) and their fighter strength consisted of only sixteen Sea Hurricanes and four Fulmars. The convoy was quickly spotted by German reconnaissance aircraft, although it was not until dawn on the 14th that the first attacks from aircraft based on Sardinia developed and these were beaten off without loss. However, at 1130 a simultaneous low-level torpedo and high-level bombing attack by almost forty aircraft escorted by twenty fighters broke through the defences and sank the freighter *Tanimbar* (8,600 tons) and severely damaged the cruiser *Liverpool*, which then had to be taken in tow by the destroyer *Antelope*. Around 1820, a formation of Ju 88s attempted to get at the carriers but was fought off by the Fleet Air Arm fighters. Later that evening, another major air attack was launched from Sicily-based aircraft of Fliegerkorps

II supported by Italian torpedo bombers. Despite the weight of the attack, no damage was inflicted and by the end of the day, the carrier fighters claimed to have shot down seventeen enemy aircraft for the loss of seven of their own and AA fire had accounted for others.

By now it was night and the convoy was entering the narrow waters of the Skerki Channel just off the north-east coast of Tunisia. At this point, the covering force under Admiral Curteis broke off as planned since the capital ships and priceless aircraft carriers could not be risked in the narrows between Sicily and the North African coast. Unexpectedly, the convoy had a relatively quiet passage through the night, staying close to the Tunisian coast so as to keep as far as possible from the Sicilian airfields. At dawn on the 15th, the convoy was 30 miles south of the small island of Pantelleria and only twelve hours out from Malta. Air cover would be provided over this final leg of the voyage by long-range Malta-based Beaufighters, later to be supplemented by Spitfires as the distance lessened. However, any thoughts that the worst was now over were rudely shattered at 0630 when a force of Italian light cruisers and several destroyers was sighted dead ahead. These were the 7th Division (*Eugenio di Savoia* and *Raimondo Montecuccoli*) under the command of Division Admiral Alberto da Zara, who had sailed from Palermo the previous evening and was now ideally placed to intercept and destroy the convoy. Opposing him was only the light cruiser *Cairo* which, converted for the AA role, was only armed with 4in guns, and a mixture of fleet and escort destroyers, most of which were also only armed with 4in guns. In the best traditions of the Royal Navy, Hardy instructed his ships to advance towards the enemy in order to allow the convoy to turn away. Several ships were hit, including *Cairo*, but in return the destroyers *Matchless* and *Marne* fought off two Italian destroyers attempting to get at the convoy, bringing one to a dead stop. While the two forces ran to the south, the British laying a smokescreen which the Italians were reluctant to penetrate, the now virtually defenceless convoy was set upon by Ju 87 dive-bombers from Sicily. This attack occurred during a gap between Beaufighter patrols (continuous air cover being notoriously difficult to achieve with land-based aircraft), and they made short work of the freighter *Chant* (5,600 tons) and damaged the *Kentucky* (9,300 tons), which had to be taken under tow by one of the minesweepers.

Hardy then turned back to the north-west to assist the convoy, which was still heading slowly south-eastwards towards Malta, but was followed by da Zara. It therefore became necessary for the convoy to reverse course but it now appeared only a matter of time before the Italian 6in cruisers closed the range and finished off the remaining freighters. Amazingly, at 0840, da Zara gave up the pursuit when a victory was within his grasp and he turned away to the east. Apparently he assumed that the convoy was altering course to keep clear of a minefield and he therefore decided to reposition his own ships to a point further east where he could make another attack. This respite allowed Hardy to bring the convoy and escort back into some semblance of order and he set off slowly back towards Malta, his speed restricted by the need to protect the crippled *Kentucky*. Behind him, the destroyer *Partridge* was towing the *Bedouin*, both having been damaged in the original engagement with da Zara's cruisers. Air escort was still patchy, and in the late morning another dive-bomber attack disabled the *Burdwan* (5,600 tons). With 150 miles to go, it was obvious that the convoy could not limp along at the pace of the damaged ships so Hardy ordered the crews of the *Kentucky* and *Burdwan* to be taken off and the ships sunk, while he increased to maximum speed with the remaining ships *Troilus* and *Orari*. It was fortunate that he did so because two hours later he received reports that the Italian cruisers had reappeared astern and were attacking the ships left to finish off the damaged merchantmen. Fortunately for the rest of the convoy, after finishing off the two freighters and damaging the minesweeper *Hebe*, da Zara was distracted by the appearance of *Bedouin* and *Partridge* still coming up from the west and turned away to engage them. The *Bedouin* was sunk but *Partridge* eventually managed to escape and made it back to Gibraltar. However, this diversion had now taken da Zara too far away from the convoy to have any hope of catching it and he therefore set course back to Palermo. The remaining ships and the two precious freighters bringing some 15,000 tons of supplies eventually made Malta after nightfall.

The old battleship HMS Malaya *was the only capital ship available for the Harpoon covering force.* (ASM)

The cruiser HMS Liverpool *was an early casualty. Damaged by an aerial torpedo, she had to be towed back to Gibraltar.* (NARA)

The force confronting the Harpoon convoy included the fast Italian light cruiser Raimondo Montecuccoli. (ASM)

The destroyer HMS Partridge *took the damaged HMS* Bedouin *under tow but had to abandon her when set upon by the two Italian cruisers and was lucky to escape back to Gibraltar.* (NARA)

OPERATION VIGOROUS: Given the fierce opposition encountered together with one of the rare instances of the Italian Navy operating effectively in co-ordination with air attacks, the outcome of Harpoon must be judged a success despite the losses incurred. Unfortunately, in terms of supplies delivered, the Vigorous convoy in the eastern Mediterranean was a total failure. During 14 June, the convoy of eleven ships escorted by cruisers and destroyers under Rear Admiral Vian had fought off no fewer than seven separate air attacks and had lost only one freighter, but others had been damaged or detached for various reasons so that only eight were left. As night fell, the convoy was subjected to probing attacks by German E-boats and he was also aware, from Ultra intercepts, that a major portion of the Italian fleet including the battleships *Littorio* and *Vittorio Veneto* was at sea and in a position to engage him in the morning. In consultation with the C-in-C (Admiral Harwood) ashore at Alexandria, it was decided that the convoy would reverse course at 0200, but executing this complicated manoeuvre gave the E-boats the chance they were looking for. The destroyer *Hasty* was sunk and the cruiser *Newcastle* damaged by a torpedo. At dawn on the 15th, RAF Beauforts attacked the Italian fleet and put a torpedo into the heavy cruiser *Trento*. In the meantime, the convoy was ordered to turn back towards Malta in the hope that further air and submarine attacks would cause the Italians to break off their sortie. When it became apparent that this was not happening, Vian was again ordered to reverse course to the east but later in the morning another destroyer was sunk by air attack and the cruiser *Birmingham* put out of action by near misses. At 1345, Vian received yet another order to turn back for Malta but, based on his own assessment of the situation, he decided not to comply and continued eastwards. This decision was entirely justified as subsequent air attacks failed to inflict further damage on the Italian ships and his own ships continued to be harassed by German dive-bombers, causing AA ammunition to be used up at prodigious rates. When, at 1500, the Italian fleet turned northwards to avoid the possibility of a night action, there was a slim chance that the convoy might get through after all. However, a cold-blooded review of ammunition and fuel stocks revealed this to be impracticable and the convoy was ordered to continue on its easterly course and return to Alexandria. On the way, the cruiser *Hermione* was torpedoed and sunk by a U-boat and the destroyer *Nestor* sank as a result of earlier damage sustained in an air attack. On the Italian side, the cruiser *Trento* was finished off by the British submarine *Umbra* and the *Littorio* was damaged by a torpedo dropped by an RAF Wellington.

HMS Coventry, *a C class cruiser converted for the AA role, was part of the escort for the Vigorous convoy. Sister ship HMS* Cairo *was with the Harpoon convoy and despite only being armed with 4in guns was in action against the Italian cruisers.* (ASM)

HMAS Nizam *was an Australian-manned N class destroyer which took part in Operation Vigorous. A sister ship, HMAS* Nestor, *was also present but was sunk by Italian aircraft on 15 June as the convoy was returning to Alexandria.* (NARA)

The Italian Navigatori class destroyer Antonio Pigafetta *was part of the surface force which would have intercepted the Vigorous convoy had it not turned back. (ASM)*

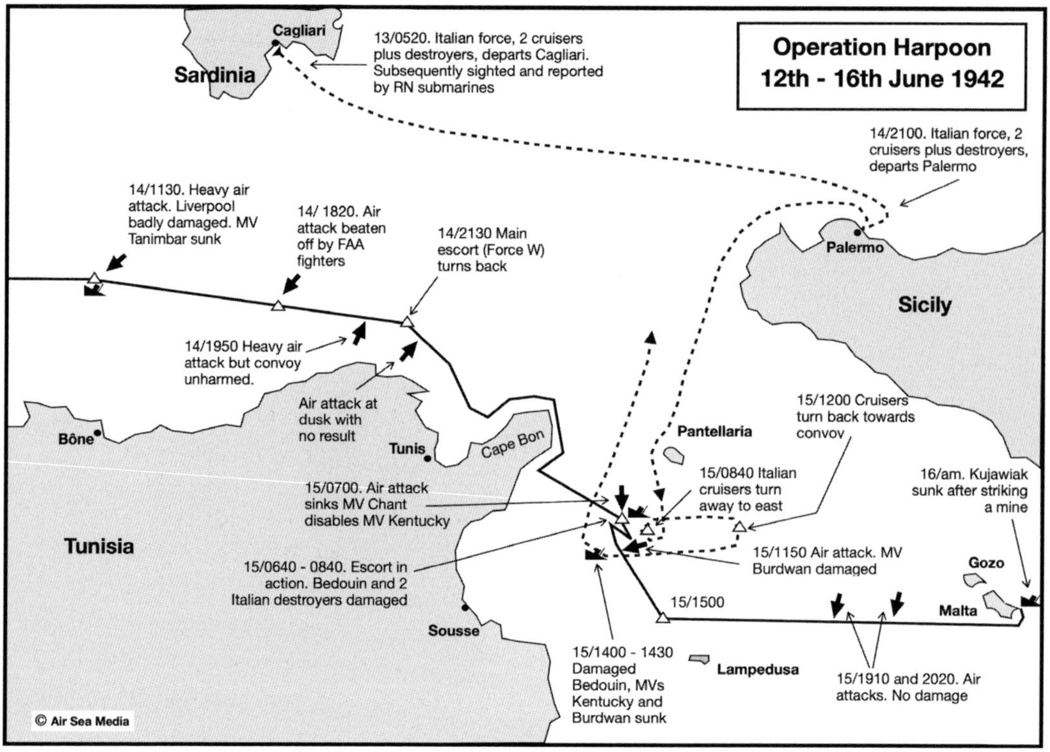
Operation Harpoon
12th - 16th June 1942
Cagliari
Sardinia
13/0520. Italian force, 2 cruisers plus destroyers, departs Cagliari. Subsequently sighted and reported by RN submarines
14/2100. Italian force, 2 cruisers plus destroyers, departs Palermo
14/1130. Heavy air attack. Liverpool badly damaged. MV Tanimbar sunk
14/ 1820. Air attack beaten off by FAA fighters
14/2130 Main escort (Force W) turns back
Palermo
Sicily
14/1950 Heavy air attack but convoy unharmed.
Air attack at dusk with no result
Bône
Tunis
Cape Bon
Pantellaria
15/1200 Cruisers turn back towards convoy
15/0840 Italian cruisers turn away to east
16/am. Kujawiak sunk after striking a mine
15/0700. Air attack sinks MV Chant disables MV Kentucky
Tunisia
15/1150 Air attack. MV Burdwan damaged
Gozo
15/0640 - 0840. Escort in action. Bedouin and 2 Italian destroyers damaged
15/1500
Malta
Sousse
15/1400 - 1430 Damaged Bedouin, MVs Kentucky and Burdwan sunk
Lampedusa
15/1910 and 2020. Air attacks. No damage
© Air Sea Media

(ASM)

Of the sixteen transports originally destined for Malta, only two got through and several warships had been sunk or damaged. The Italian Navy claimed a victory, which it was in tactical terms, but the two ships that did get through were just enough to keep the island going while a further relief effort was organised. In the event, the 15,000 tons of supplies made the vital difference that kept Malta going for another few weeks in its darkest hour.

Operation Pedestal

Date: 10 to 15 August 1942
Location: Western Mediterranean

Allied Forces (Force H)
Commander: Vice Admiral Edward Neville Syfret RN
Ships: Aircraft carriers: *Victorious, Indomitable, Eagle, Furious.* Battleships: *Nelson, Rodney.* Cruisers: *Phoebe, Sirius, Charybdis.* Destroyers: *Laforey, Lightning, Lookout, Quentin, Eskimo, Tartar, Ithuriel, Antelope, Wishart, Vansittart, Westcott, Zetland, Wilton*

Allied Forces (Convoy Close Escort)
Commander: Rear Admiral Harold Martin Burrough RN
Ships: Cruisers: *Nigeria, Kenya, Manchester, Cairo.* Destroyers: *Ashanti, Intrepid, Icarus, Foresight, Fury, Pathfinder, Penn, Derwent, Bramham, Bicester, Ledbury*

Axis Forces
Commanders: Admiral Angelo Iachino (C-in-C Italian Fleet). Field Marshal Albert Kesselring (C-in-C German Mediterranean forces)
Ships: Cruisers: *Gorizia, Trieste, Bolzano, Eugenio di Savoia, Raimondo Montecuccoli, Muzio Attendolo.* Destroyers: *Aviere, Geniere, Camicia Nera, Legionario, Ascari, Corsaro, Grecale, Maestrale, Gioberti, Oriani, Fuciliere*
Submarines: At least nineteen Italian submarines and German U-boats deployed in the western Mediterranean
Coastal Forces: Several German and Italian motor torpedo boats (MAS and MS types)

BACKGROUND: In May and June 1942 Rommel had outfought the British 8th Army, which was forced to retreat all the way back to El Alamein. A holding battle early in July finally stopped Rommel in his tracks and gave the 8th Army time to start re-equipping and building up its strength to retake the offensive. At the same time, Malta began to build up its fighter strength and by the end of July, Royal Navy submarines were again based at Valetta, striking at Rommel's supply routes. Nevertheless, Malta was desperately short of food and fuel and unless more supplies could be got through, this brief resurgence would end and the possibility of a successful offensive by the 8th Army would inevitably have to be delayed. A further relief convoy was therefore planned for early August but it was decided to concentrate all efforts into the western Mediterranean. The lessons of the Harpoon operation were taken to heart and the most powerful Royal Navy carrier force ever assembled up to that time formed part of Force H, the covering force. The old faithful, *Eagle*, was reinforced by the modern armoured carriers *Victorious* and *Indomitable*, while the older *Furious* was attached to ferry thirty-eight Spitfires destined for Malta. Force H also included the battleships *Nelson* and *Rodney*, as well as cruisers and destroyers. The convoy close escort included the AA cruiser *Cairo*, veteran of Harpoon and other Malta convoys, but she was now backed up by the modern 6in cruisers *Nigeria*, *Kenya* and *Manchester* to counter any attack by Italian cruisers as had previously occurred. The convoy itself consisted of thirteen modern fast merchant ships (two American, the rest British) as well as the American-owned but British-manned tanker *Ohio*. Passing through the Strait of Gibraltar early on 10 August, the convoy joined up with its escorting forces and set off towards Malta. The stage was set for one of the fiercest convoy battles of the war.

THE ACTION: The convoy was located by Axis aircraft at 1010 on 11 August. Later that day, *Furious* flew off her Spitfires before turning back to Gibraltar with a destroyer escort. Almost at the same time, Lieutenant Commander Rosenbaum skilfully took the German *U-73* under the British destroyer screen and put a full salvo of four torpedoes in HMS *Eagle*. The gallant carrier rolled over and sank within eight minutes, 260 of her crew perishing as she went down. The convoy ploughed on and by evening was being attacked by Sardinian-based aircraft, which achieved no results for the loss of several aircraft. At dawn on 12 August, the convoy was still pushing on, covered by fighters from *Victorious* and *Indomitable* which broke up an early attack by nineteen Ju 88s at around 0900. A second attack involved over 100 aircraft of the Regia Aeronautica, some equipped with a new 'motobomba' circling torpedo, and also included a few Re.2001 fighters carrying a new type of heavy bomb. One of these succeeded in planting its bomb squarely on *Victorious*'s flight deck but, fortunately, it failed to explode. The Italian effort was followed up by more German dive-bombers, some of which evaded the fighters and severely damaged the freighter *Deucalion*, which fell out of line and headed towards the Tunisian coast, where it was torpedoed and sunk later that evening.

By late afternoon the convoy was approaching the Skerki Bank and the entrance to the Sicilian Channel, where the Axis submarines were lying in wait. But first there was yet another air attack to come, this time by well-drilled Ju 87 dive-bombers from Sicily synchronised with fourteen Italian torpedo bombers. In the wild mêlée that followed, *Indomitable*'s flight deck was hit three times and although the armoured deck was not penetrated, she was no longer able to operate aircraft. A torpedo hit the destroyer *Forester*, which later sank, but the remainder of the merchant ships steamed on in good order. This situation could not last and at around 2000, the convoy was torn apart by torpedoes fired from two Italian submarines (*Dessiè* and *Axum*) which hit the cruisers *Nigeria* and *Cairo*, and also the tanker *Ohio*. Destroyers raced out looking for the submarines while the convoy was thrown into disorder as ships veered off course to avoid the *Ohio*. In this state of confusion, a further air attack arrived as darkness was falling and the *Empire Hope* was hit and brought to a stop (she was later sunk) while the *Clan Ferguson* was sunk outright. Both the *Brisbane Star* and the cruiser *Kenya* were also hit by torpedoes but were soon under way again, little the worse for the damage. The *Brisbane Star*, finding herself alone, later made her own way to Malta by hugging the Tunisian shore for most of the voyage and luckily avoiding air attacks.

By now the rest of the convoy and escort was split into various groups and at midnight was off Cape Bon in the narrowest part of the Sicilian Channel. Waiting here were the fast Italian MAS boats (some German manned), which from 0100 gave the tired British crews no respite as they tore through the divided escort. An early success was the crippling of the cruiser *Manchester*, which had to be abandoned and sunk the next day. Subsequently the American *Almeria Lykes* and *Santa Elisa*, and the British *Wairangi* and *Glenorchy* were all torpedoed and sunk during the night. Also torpedoed was the *Rochester Castle* but, despite severe damage to the forward holds, she did not sink and continued on course. As indeed did the *Ohio*, whose gallant crew had eventually doused the fierce fire caused when she was torpedoed, shored up the straining bulkheads and worked the ship up to 16 knots in an effort to catch up with the other ships. Altogether, at dawn on the 13th there were only seven merchant ships in the convoy (and the *Brisbane Star* proceeding independently).

It was at this stage in the previous Harpoon convoy that the Italian cruiser squadron had appeared and, as such a force had been spotted the previous day heading south, there was no reason to expect that events would be any different on this August day. In fact, an Italian force of three heavy and three light cruisers (which should easily have finished off the convoy given the depleted state of the escort) had turned back due to lack of air cover. To make matters worse, the submarine *Unbroken* (Lieutenant Commander Alastair Mars DSO DSC) succeeded in torpedoing the cruisers *Bolzano* and *Attendolo* with one salvo of four torpedoes when they were north of the Strait of Messina. Meanwhile at 0800, the air attacks on the convoy, now some 200 miles out from Malta, began again and the *Waimarama* was hit. Her deck cargo of aviation fuel ignited and the ship blew up and sank. Some of the blazing debris fell on the *Ohio* and started a fire which was only put out after a long struggle. The tanker now seemed to become the focus of the enemy's attacks and one dive-bomber actually crashed into her, while several near misses wrecked her machinery and the ship came to a halt. During this attack the *Rochester Castle* was hit again but was able to continue, and the *Dorset* was stopped by hits from several bombs. The destroyer *Bramham* stood by the *Dorset* while the *Penn* took the *Ohio* in tow until further damage caused her to be abandoned at 1400. She was later reboarded and at one stage got under way at around 5 knots but this effort had to be abandoned when another dive-bombing attack put a bomb in the engine room. By the end of the day, the *Port Chalmers*, *Rochester Castle* and *Melbourne Star* had reached the safety of Valetta harbour to a frenzied welcome from the island's populace and servicemen. During the night, the *Penn*, assisted by the minesweeper *Rye* and the destroyer *Ledbury*, again got the crippled tanker moving and they were later joined by the *Bramham* after the *Dorset* had been finally sunk by three bombs.

On the morning of the 14th, the *Ohio* was still being taken slowly towards her destination when another attack by Ju 88s developed. This was broken up by Spitfires from Malta and proved to be the last attack as the ships were now within easy range of the Malta fighters. Only by the superhuman efforts and exemplary seamanship of all concerned was the floating wreck of the *Ohio*, and her precious cargo of 10,000 tons of oil fuel, finally brought safely into Valetta. Including her, and the *Brisbane Star*, which also arrived on the 14th, a total of five ships had reached Malta, bringing with them enough supplies to ensure that the island would not only survive, but thrive as an offensive base until the end of the year. By then, the Axis forces in North Africa would be defeated and the Mediterranean would be much more open to Allied shipping, although it was not until 20 November, when a convoy of four merchant ships from Alexandria (Operation Stone Age) reached Malta without loss, that the island's long ordeal could at last be considered at an end.

For Operation Pedestal the Royal Navy fielded no fewer than four aircraft carriers, including HMS Furious, *which was ferrying Spitfires for Malta. Here HMS* Indomitable *and HMS* Eagle *follow astern of HMS* Victorious. *Unfortunately, HMS* Eagle *was sunk by a U-boat attack on 11 August.* (WC)

Between them the carriers embarked no fewer than seventy fighters, including eighteen Fairey Fulmars of 809 and 884 NAS aboard HMS Victorious. *By 1942 the two-seat Fulmar was obsolete and lacked the performance of the single-seat Sea Hurricanes and Martlets. Nevertheless, they had some success against the attacking German and Italian bombers.* (NARA)

Above: *HMS* Indomitable *carried a total of fifty-four aircraft compared to a nominal capacity of only thirty-six aboard HMS* Victorious. *Unfortunately,* Indomitable's *flight deck was put out of action after an air attack on the evening of 12 August, leaving* Victorious *as the only operational carrier.* (NARA)

Left: *The Italian SM.79 three-engined torpedo bombers were flown with great skill and courage and succeeded in sinking some of the ships in the convoy. However, this example is in a dramatic fatal dive after being disabled by AA fire from the escorting warships.* (AC)

The Hunt class destroyer HMS Ledbury *formed part of the convoy's close escort. She was involved in picking up survivors from the MV* Waimarama *and also searched for survivors from the cruiser* Manchester. *Hastening to join the convoy, she came across the crippled tanker* Ohio *and played a major part in the subsequent saga to save the ship and her vital cargo.* (NARA)

Following the serious damage to the cruiser HMS Nigeria, *Rear Admiral Borrough commanding the close escort transferred his flag to the destroyer HMS* Ashanti. (NARA)

HMS Pathfinder *was one of the P class destroyers optimised for the AA role with a main armament of 4in guns. As such she was a very useful addition to the close escort.* (NARA)

Afloat only by virtue of being lashed to the destroyers Penn *and* Bramham, *the oil tanker* Ohio *slowly makes her way over the final stages of her epic voyage to Malta.* (AC)

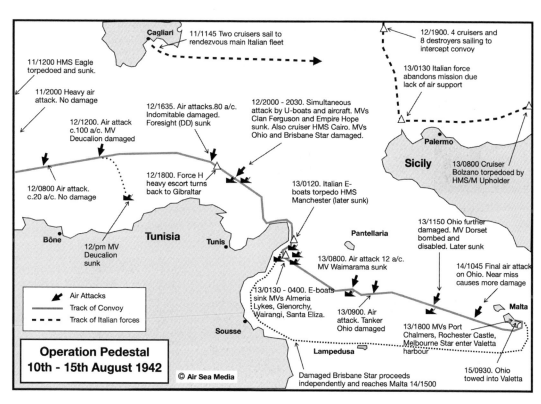

11/1145 Two cruisers sail to rendezvous main Italian fleet

12/1900. 4 cruisers and 8 destroyers sailing to intercept convoy

13/0130 Italian force abandons mission due lack of air support

11/1200 HMS Eagle torpedoed and sunk.

11/2000 Heavy air attack. No damage

12/1200. Air attack c.100 a/c. MV Deucalion damaged

12/1635. Air attacks.80 a/c. Indomitable damaged. Foresight (DD) sunk

12/2000 - 2030. Simultaneous attack by U-boats and aircraft. MVs Clan Ferguson and Empire Hope sunk. Also cruiser HMS Cairo. MVs Ohio and Brisbane Star damaged.

Palermo

13/0800 Cruiser Bolzano torpedoed by HMS/M Upholder

Sicily

12/0800 Air attack. c.20 a/c. No damage

12/1800 Force H heavy escort turns back to Gibraltar

13/0120. Italian E-boats torpedo HMS Manchester (later sunk)

13/1150 Ohio further damaged. MV Dorset bombed and disabled. Later sunk

Bône

Tunisia

Tunis

Pantellaria

12/pm MV Deucalion sunk

13/0800. Air attack 12 a/c. MV Waimarama sunk

14/1045 Final air attack on Ohio. Near miss causes more damage

Malta

Air Attacks

Track of Convoy

Track of Italian forces

13/0130 - 0400. E-boats sink MVs Almeria Lykes, Glenorchy, Wairangi, Santa Eliza.

13/0900. Air attack. Tanker Ohio damaged

13/1800 MVs Port Chalmers, Rochester Castle, Melbourne Star enter Valetta harbour

Operation Pedestal 10th - 15th August 1942

© Air Sea Media

Sousse

Lampedusa

15/0930. Ohio towed into Valetta

Damaged Brisbane Star proceeds independently and reaches Malta 14/1500

(ASM)

Naval Battle of Casablanca (Operation Torch)

Date: 8 to 11 November 1942
Location: Casablanca, Morocco. Atlantic coast

Allied Forces (US Navy)

Commander: Rear Admiral Henry Kent Hewitt USN (Commander
                Task Force 34.9)
Ships: Aircraft carriers: *Ranger* (CV4), *Sangamon*, *Suwannee*,
                Chenango, *Santee*. Battleship: *Massachusetts*. Cruisers:
                Augusta, *Wichita*, *Tuscaloosa*, *Brooklyn*. Destroyers:
                Mayrant, *Rhind*, *Wainwright*, *Jenkins*, *Rowan*, *Woolsey*,
                Ludlow, *Edison*, *Wilkes*, *Swanson*, *Bristol*, *Boyle*,
                Murphy, *Tillman*

Vichy French Forces

Commander: Rear Admiral Félix Michelier
Ships: Battleship: *Jean Bart*. Cruiser: *Primauguet*. Destroyers:
                Albatros, *Milan*, *L'Alcyon*, *Boulonnais*, *Brestois*, *Fougueux*,
                Frondeur, *Simoun*, *Tempête*. Submarines: *Le Tonnant*,
                La Sybille, *Le Conquérant*, *La Psyché*, *Méduse*, *Orphée*,
                Oréade, *Amphritrite*, *Amazone*, *Antiope*, *Sidi-Ferruch*

BACKGROUND: Provoked by the Japanese attack on Pearl Harbor, the United States entered the war on 7 December 1941. Almost immediately, an Anglo-American Joint Chiefs of Staff organisation was set up to oversee the strategic direction of the war and despite a natural desire by the Americans to avenge the Japanese attack, a policy of 'Germany First' was agreed. The preferred American strategy was to launch an offensive against North West Europe using the British Isles as a springboard at the earliest opportunity (possibly in 1942 and certainly by 1943). The British point of view, while agreeing in principle, was that such an operation would not be feasible until 1944 at the earliest due to logistic and other considerations and they preferred to concentrate on North Africa and the Mediterranean before advancing into southern Europe. Nevertheless, the Americans (notably President Roosevelt) were very eager to see their ground troops in action before the end of 1942, and so, after much debate, it was agreed at a relatively late stage that joint Anglo–American landings would take place on North Africa during November 1942. Codenamed Operation Torch, the overall plan allowed for British-led (from the naval point of view) landings at Oran and Algiers while an all-American task force would land on the French Moroccan Atlantic coast with the objective of securing the port of Casablanca before moving on to join up with the other forces and advancing into Tunisia.

From a military point of view these were sound objectives but politically it was fraught with difficulty. The territories to be attacked were administered by Vichy France, which technically was now a neutral country. Relationships between Britain and France were already strained due to the action at Oran in June 1940 where French sailors had been killed by the action of the Royal Navy. Consequently it was decided that the whole operation would be presented as being under American command, a move which it was hoped would be more likely to persuade Vichy French forces to lay down their arms and side with the Allied cause. In addition, US officers and politicians were landed by submarine for secret discussions with French officers thought to be sympathetic to the Allied cause. The US troop convoy sailed from Chesapeake Bay on 23 October and was in position off the Moroccan coast on the night of 7 November, while at the same time, the other invasion forces which had sailed from Britain were then passing through the Strait of Gibraltar prior to assaulting their objectives the following morning.

THE ACTION: The American Western Task Force (TF34) assault on the Atlantic coast of French Morocco had three separate objectives. The Northern group (TF34.8) landed against stiff French opposition at Mehedia, their objective being the capture of the airfield inland at Port Lyautey, which was taken early on 10 November, and US P-40 fighters flown in from the escort carrier USS *Chenango* were using the airfield by 1030 that day. The Southern (TF34.10) group's objective was the small port of Safi, some 150 south of Casablanca, which was the only place where tanks of the US 2nd Armoured Division could be offloaded. At that stage of the war specialised Tank Landing Ships (LST) were not available and the tanks were carried in the USS *Lakehurst*, a converted train ferry. Despite opposition from shore batteries, the initial assault was successful and *Lakehurst* was able to start discharging her cargo on the afternoon of the 8th.

The Centre (TF34.9) group's objective was the major port of Casablanca, whose capture was essential to the whole American campaign in North Africa. It was heavily defended by shore batteries supported by 15in guns of the battleship *Jean Bart* moored in the harbour. She had escaped from France in June 1940 in an incomplete state with only the forward quadruple 15in gun turret mounted and Casablanca lacked the facilities for any further major work. In addition, there was the light cruiser *Primauguet*, nine destroyers and several submarines, most of which attempted to engage the American ships offshore and provoked the unusual spectacle of a naval battle centred on an amphibious assault.

At dawn on the 8th, the waves of landing craft approached the beach at Fedhala, just north of Casablanca, while fire from the cruiser *Brooklyn* silenced the Pont Blondin battery at the northern end of the beach The battleship *Massachusetts* and other cruisers (part of TF34.1 covering force) engaged other batteries at El Hank to the south while air support was provided by the carrier USS *Ranger* (CV4) stationed offshore. A combination of gunfire from the battleship and air attacks temporarily put the *Jean Bart* out of action but in the meantime Admiral Michelier ordered his destroyers, followed by the cruiser *Primauguet*, to sortie against the transports massed off the Fedhala beachhead.

First to engage, around 0900, were the destroyers *Milan*, *Fougueux* and *Boulonnais*, which managed to sink one landing craft and damage a destroyer but were subjected to attacks by *Ranger*'s aircraft and gunfire from the USS *Wichita* and USS *Tuscaloosa* as well as the escorting American destroyers. A running fight developed, with the French destroyers laying smokescreens, despite which the *Fougueux* was sunk and heavily damaged *Milan* was beached and abandoned, while *Boulonnais* turned back towards the harbour. In the meantime the cruiser *Primauguet*, accompanied by destroyers *Albatros*, *Brestois* and *Frodeur*, came out but were met with sustained and accurate fire from *Massachusetts* and the cruisers, and were forced to turn back, with *Albatros* also being run ashore in a sinking condition. *Primauguet* was badly damaged and was beached in the harbour, where she subsequently burnt out, while the other two destroyers capsised and sank. By midday the USS *Augusta* had also caught and sunk the *Boulonnais*, which had survived the initial action.

At the start of the day there were eleven French submarines in the harbour and three of these were sunk at their moorings by gunfire or air attack, while of the remainder, only four managed to launch attacks on the American ships, all unsuccessful, and at least one was sunk by destroyer counter-attacks. Due to poor weather there was little naval action on the 9th but the following day two French minesweepers sortied with the intention of shelling the Fedhala beachhead. They were supported by the heavy guns of the *Jean Bart*, these having been repaired by French engineers. However, this was not enough to overcome the American support force offshore and the minesweepers turned back having accomplished nothing. SBD dive-bombers from the USS *Ranger* then attacked the *Jean Bart* and put her out of action for the rest of the battle.

During the day plans were laid for further landings at Casablanca on the 11th to support the troops already ashore and to capture and put out of action the troublesome battery at El Hank. However, the fighting was brought to a sudden conclusion by a ceasefire ordered by the French commander in North Africa, Admiral Darlan. Subsequently, honour satisfied, the French authorities immediately entered into co-operation with the Allied forces and the port facilities (now badly damaged) at Casablanca were made available. The fighting had cost the French Navy a light cruiser, four destroyers and five submarines as well as number of smaller craft. No less than 462 naval personnel were killed. Up to this point damage to American ships was very light although many landing craft had been lost due to the sea conditions off Fedhala. However, even though the French had accepted a ceasefire, the Germans had not. Over the next two days the submarines *U-173* and *U-130* sank four US troopships and damaged a destroyer and an oiler, although *U-173* was subsequently sunk by the US destroyers *Quick*, *Swanson* and *Woolsey* off Casablanca on 16 November.

The Torch landings in North Africa, together with the earlier British victory at El Alamein at the end of October, marked a turning point in the war and the Allied cause at last began to gather some momentum against the hitherto invincible German Army, although it was not until May 1943 that the North African campaign was finally completed. With Axis forces cleared out of Africa, and later from Sicily and southern Italy, it became possible to route shipping through the Mediterranean and the Suez Canal rather than the much longer route around the Cape into the Indian Ocean. This effectively released shipping for other strategic tasks, notably the build-up of US and Canadian forces in the UK in preparation for the great assault on North West Europe, which eventually occurred on 6 June 1944.

The quarterdeck of the USS Massachusetts *(BB59) during a lull in the action. Note the prominent Stars and Stripes flown at the mainmast in the vain hope that the Vichy forces would not oppose an American landing.* (NHIC)

The heavy cruiser USS Tuscaloosa *(CA37) played an active role as part of the covering force, engaging shore batteries and countering sorties by the French destroyers.* (NARA)

Douglas SBD Dauntless dive-bombers of VS-41operating from the carrier USS Ranger *(CV4) provided air support during the action. In particular they attacked and damaged the battleship* Jean Bart, *and hit the cruiser* Primauguet *with at least two bombs.* (NARA)

The incomplete French battleship Jean Bart *put up a spirited resistance with her only functioning 15in gun turret, which was only temporarily put out of action by a bomb dropped by an SBD dive-bomber. In this view, taken after the action, the damage to the bow caused by air attacks is visible.* (NARA)

The French 2,400-tonne destroyer Albatros *fought valiantly throughout the morning but just before noon she was put out of action by Dauntless dive-bombers of VS-41 and subsequently beached.* (NARA)

The destroyer USS Swanson *(DD443) was one of three destroyers that engaged the initial sortie by the French destroyers and attempted to lead them away from the vulnerable landing craft.* (NARA)

The transport anchorage off the landing beaches at Fedhala was protected by the cruisers USS Augusta *(CA31) and USS* Brooklyn *(CL40). The former, shown here, also carried the commander of the land forces, Major General George S. Patton.* (NARA)

Aftermath of the battle. In the foreground are the beached destroyers Albatros *(X73) and* Milan *(X111) while the badly damaged cruiser* Primauguet *is anchored behind them (she was subsequently scrapped).* (NARA)

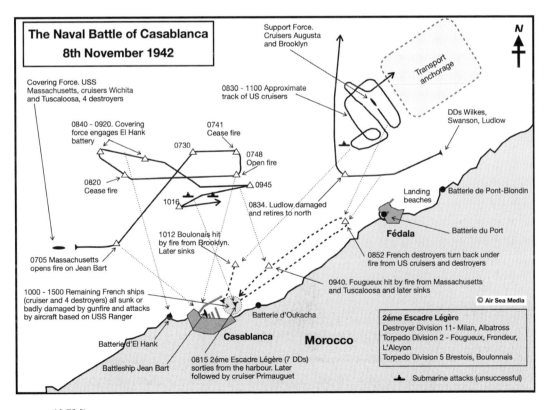

The Naval Battle of Casablanca
8th November 1942

N

Support Force.
Cruisers Augusta
and Brooklyn

Transport anchorage

Covering Force. USS
Massachusetts, cruisers Wichita
and Tuscaloosa, 4 destroyers

0830 - 1100 Approximate
track of US cruisers

DDs Wilkes,
Swanson, Ludlow

0840 - 0920. Covering
force engages El Hank
battery

0741
Cease fire

0730

0748
Open fire

0820
Cease fire

0945

0834. Ludlow damaged
and retires to north

1016

Landing
beaches

Batterie de Pont-Blondin

1012 Boulonais hit
by fire from Brooklyn.
Later sinks

Fédala

Batterie du Port

0705 Massachusetts
opens fire on Jean Bart

0852 French destroyers turn back under
fire from US cruisers and destroyers

1000 - 1500 Remaining French ships
(cruiser and 4 destroyers) all sunk or
badly damaged by gunfire and attacks
by aircraft based on USS Ranger

0940. Fougueux hit by fire from Massachusetts
and Tuscaloosa and later sinks

© Air Sea Media

Batterie d'Oukacha

Casablanca

Morocco

Batterie d'El Hank

Battleship Jean Bart

0815 2éme Escadre Légère (7 DDs)
sorties from the harbour. Later
followed by cruiser Primauguet

2éme Escadre Légère
Destroyer Division 11- Milan, Albatross
Torpedo Division 2 - Fougueux, Frondeur,
L'Alcyon
Torpedo Division 5 Brestois, Boulonnais

⚓ Submarine attacks (unsuccessful)

(ASM)

(Editorial note: Although this action took place off the Atlantic coast of French Morocco, the above narrative has been included in the section dealing with the Mediterranean as the American operation was part of the much larger Operation Torch, which included landings on the North African Mediterranean coast, and was closely related to the overall strategy in that theatre).

Appendix

List of Warships

The following list gives brief details of warships (apart from submarines) mentioned in the battle narratives in this book. The abbreviations used are listed in the glossary.

Ship	Type	Navy	Tonnage	Kts	Armament
A. Pigafetta	DD	It.N	1,940	38	6 x 4.7in, 2 x 37mm, 8 x 20mm, 6 TT
Abruzzi	CL	It.N	9,960	35	10 x 6in, 8 x 3.9in, 8 x 37mm, 6 TT
Acasta	DD	RN	1,350	35	4 x 4.7in, 2 x 2pdr, 8 TT
Achates	DD	RN	1,350	35	4 x 4.7in, 2 x 2pdr, 8 TT
Achilles	CL	RNZN	7,200	32	8 x 6in, 8 x 4in, 8 TT
Active	DD	RN	1,350	35	4 x 4.7in, 2 x 2pdr, 8 TT
Admiral Hipper	CA	Ger	13,900	32	8 x 8in, 12 x 4.1in 12 TT
Admiral Scheer	Pzs	Ger	12,100	26	6 x 11in, 8 x 5.9in, 6 x 4.1in, 8 TT, 2 a/c
Airedale	DE	RN	1,050	27	4 x 4in, 4 x 2pdr, 2 TT
Ajax	CL	RN	7,200	32	8 x 6in, 8 x 4in, 8 TT
Albatros	DD	Fra	2,441	36	5 x 5.5in, 4 x 37mm, 6 TT
Aldenham	DE	RN	1.050	27	4 x 4in, 4 x 2pdr, 2 TT
Alfieri	DD	It.N	1,700	39	4 x 4.7in, 2 x 37mm, 6 TT
Alpino	DD	It.N	1,800	39	5 x 4.7, 1 x 37mm, 6 TT
Amagiri	DD	IJN	2,090	34	6 x 5in, 9 x 24in TT
Amatsukaze	DD	IJN	2,033	35	6 x 5in, 8 x 24in TT
Andrea Doria	BB	It.N	26,000	27	10 x 12.6in, 12 x 5.3in, 10 x 3.5in
Antelope	DD	RN	1,350	35	4 x 4.7in, 2 x 2pdr, 8 TT
Anton Schmitt	DD	Ger	2,410	38	5 x 5in, 8 TT
Ardent	DD	RN	1,350	35	4 x 4.7in, 2 x 2pdr, 8 TT
Arethusa	CL	RN	5,250	32	6 x 6in, 8 x 4in, 6 TT, 1 a/c
Argus	CV	RN	14,555	20	4 x 4in AA, 20 a/c
Ark Royal	CV	RN	22,000	30	16 x 4.5in, 48 x 2pdr, 72 a/c
Ascari	DD	It.N	1,800	39	5 x 4.7, 1 x 37mm, 6 TT

Ship	Type	Navy	Tonnage	Kts	Armament
Ashanti	DD	RN	1,960	36	8 X 4.7in, 4 TT
Augusta	CA	USN	9.050	32	9 x 8in, 8 x 5in, 2 x 3pdr, 4 a/c
Aurora	CL	RN	5,250	32	6 x 6in, 8 x 4in, 6 TT
Australia	CA	RAN	10,500	31	8 x 8in, 8 x 4in, 8 x 2pdr, 8 TT, 1 a/c
Aviere	DD	It.N	1,800	39	5 x 4.7, 1 x 37mm, 6 TT
Avon Vale	DE	RN	1.050	27	6 x 4in, 4 x 2pdr
Badsworth	DE	RN	1.050	27	6 x 4in, 4 x 2pdr
Bande Nere	CL	It.N	5,200	37	8 x 6in, 6 x 3.9in, 4 TT, 2 a/c
Barham	BB	RN	31,100	24	8 x 15in, 12 x 6in, 8 x 4in, 1 a/c
Bartolomeo Colleoni	CL	It.N	5,200	37	8 x 6in, 6 x 3.9in, 4 TT, 2 a/c
Beaufort	DE	RN	1.050	27	6 x 4in, 4 x 2pdr
Bedouin	DD	RN	1,960	36	8 x 4.7in, 4 TT
Belfast	CL	RN	10,260	32	12 x 6in, 12 x 4in, 6 TT, 2 a/c
Bernd von Arnim	DD	Ger	2,250	38	5 x 5in 8 TT
Bersagliere	DD	It.N	1,800	39	5 x 4.7, 1 x 37mm, 6 TT
Berwick	CA	RN	10,500	31	8 x 8in, 8 x 4in, 8 x 2pdr, 8 TT, 1 a/c
Bicester	DE	RN	1.050	27	6 x 4in, 4 x 2pdr
Birmingham	CL	RN	9,100	32	12x 6in, 8 x 4in, 6 TT, 2 a/c
Bismarck	BB	Ger	41,700	29	8 x 15in, 12 x 5.9in, 16 x 4.1in, 6 a/c
Biter	CVE	RN	12,150	17	1. x 5in, 2 x 3in, 10 x 20mm, 20 a/c
Blankney	DE	RN	1.050	27	6 x 4in, 4 x 2pdr
Bolzano	CA	It.N	11,000	36	8 x 8in, 12 x 3.9in, 8 TT, 3 a/c
Boulonnais	DD	Fra	1,378	33	4 x 5.1in, 2 x 37mm, 6 TT
Boyle	DD	USN	1,620	37	4 x 5in 5 TT
Bramble	MS	RN	850	16	1 x 4in, 8 x 20mm
Bramham	DE	RN	1.050	27	6 x 4in, 4 x 2pdr
Brestois	DD	Fra	1,378	33	4 x 5.1in, 2 x 37mm, 6 TT
Bretagne	BB	Fra	22,200	21	10 x 13.4in, 14 x 5.5in, 4 a/c
Bristol	DD	USN	1,630	37	4 x 5in 10 TT
Brooklyn	CL	USN	10,000	34	15 x 6in, 8 x 5in, 4 x 3pdr, 4 a/c
Caio Duilio	BB	It.N	26,000	27	10 x 12.6in, 12 x 5.3in, 10 x 3.5in
Cairo	CL	RN	1.050	27	6 x 4in, 4 x 2pdr
Camicia Nera	DD	It.N	1,800	39	5 x 4.7, 1 x 37mm, 6 TT
Campbell	DD	RN	1,530	36	5 x 4.7in, 1 x 3in, 6 TT

Ship	Type	Navy	Tonnage	Kts	Armament
Carabiniere	DD	It.N	1,800	39	5 x 4.7, 1 x 37mm, 6 TT
Carducci	DD	It.N	1,700	39	4 x 4.7in, 2 x 37mm, 6 TT
Carlisle	CL	RN	4,290	27	8 x 4in, 4 x 2pdr
Charybdis	CL	RN	5,600	33	8 x 4.5in, 8 x 20mm, 6 TT
Chenango	CVE	USN	11,400	18	2 x 5in, 8 x 40mm, 30 a/c
Cleopatra	CL	RN	5,600	33	10 x 5.25in, 8 x 2pdr, 6 TT
Commandant Teste	CVS	Fra	10,000	20	12 x 3.9in, 26 a/c
Conte di Cavour	BB	It.N	26,140	27	10 x 12.6in, 12 x 4.7in, 8 x 3.9in
Corazziere	DD	It.N	1,800	39	5 x 4.7in, 1 x 37mm, 6 TT
Corsaro	DD	It.N	1,830	39	5 x 4.7in, 6 TT
Cossack	DD	RN	1,960	36	8 X 4.7in, 4 TT
Coventry	CL	RN	4,190	27	10 x 4in, 8 x 2pdr
Cumberland	CA	RN	10,800	31	8 x 8in, 8 x 4in, 8 x 2 pdr, 8 TT, 2 a/c
Croome	DE	RN	1.050	27	6 x 4in, 4 x 2pdr
Da Recco	DD	It.N	1,940	38	6 x 4.7in, 2 x 37mm, 8 x 20mm, 6 TT
De Ruyter	CL	Neth	6,450	32	7 x 5.9in, 10 x 40mm, 2 a/c
Derwent	DE	RN	1,050	27	4 x 4in, 4 x 2pdr, 2 TT
Devonshire	CA	RN	9,850	32	8 x 8in, 8 x 4in, 8 TT 1 a/c
Dianella	PF	RN	925	16	1 x 4in, 1 x 2pdr
Dido	CL	RN	5,660	33	10 x 5.25in, 8 x 2pdr, 6 TT
Diether von Roeder	DD	Ger	2,410	38	5 x 5in, 8 TT
Duca d'Aosta	CL	It.N	8,660	37	8 x 6in, 6 x 3.9in, 4 TT, 2 a/c
Duke of York	BB	RN	35,000	29	10 X 14in, 16 X 5.25in
Dulverton	DE	RN	1.050	27	6 x 4in, 4 x 2pdr
Dunkerque	BB	Fra	26,500	30	8 x 13in, 16 x 5.1in, 4 a/c
Dyson	DD	USN	2,050	37	5 x 5in, 10 TT
E. Pessagno	DD	It.N	1,940	38	6 x 4.7in, 2 x 37mm, 8 x 20mm, 6 TT
Eagle	CV	RN	22,600	24	9 x 6in, 4 x 4in, 24 a/c
Edison	DD	USN	1,630	37	5 x 5in, 10 TT
Electra	DD	RN	1,405	35	4 x 4.7in, 8 TT
Encounter	DD	RN	1,405	35	4 x 4.7in, 8 TT
Enterprise	CL	RN	7,550	33	7 x 6in, 3 x 4in, 1 a/c
Erich Koellner	DD	Ger	2,250	38	5 x 5in, 8 TT
Erich Giese	DD	Ger	2,250	38	5 x 5in, 8 TT

Ship	Type	Navy	Tonnage	Kts	Armament
Eridge	DE	RN	1.050	27	6 x 4in, 4 x 2pdr
Escapade	DD	RN	1,405	35	4 x 4.7in, 8 TT
Escort	DD	RN	1,405	35	4 x 4.7in, 8 TT
Eskimo	DD	RN	1,960	36	8 X 4.7in, 4 TT
Eugenio di Savoia	CL	It.N	9,000	37	8 x 6in, 6 x 3.9in, 4 TT, 2 a/c
Euro	DD	It.N	1,090	36	4 x 4.7in, 6 TT
Euryalus	CL	RN	5,660	33	10 x 5.25in, 8 x 2pdr, 6 TT
Exeter	CA	RN	8,390	32	6 x 8in, 4 x 4in, 6 TT, 1 a/c
Exmoor	DE	RN	1.050	27	4 x 4in, 4 x 2pdr
Express	DD	RN	1,405	35	4 x 4.7in, 8 TT
Falke	TB	Ger	924	33	3 x 4.1in, 6 TT
Faulknor	DD	RN	1,475	35	5 x 4.7in, 8 TT
Fearless	DD	RN	1,405	35	4 x 4.7in, 8 TT
Fiume	CA	It.N	11,500	32	8 x 8in, 12 x 3.9in, 2 a/c
Folgore	DD	It.N	1,238	38	4 x 4.7in, 6 TT
Foresight	DD	RN	1,405	35	4 x 4.7in, 8 TT
Forester	DD	RN	1,405	35	4 x 4.7in, 8 TT
Formidable	CV	RN	23,200	30	16 x 4.5in, 36 – 54 a/c
Fortune	DD	RN	1,405	35	4 x 4.7in, 8 TT
Fougueux	DD	Fra	1,378	33	4 x 5.1in, 2 x 37mm, 6 TT
Foxhound	DD	RN	1,405	35	4 x 4.7in, 8 TT
Friedrich Eckholdt	DD	Ger	2,171	38	5 x 5in, 4 x 37mm, 8 TT
Friedrich Ihn	DD	Ger	2,171	38	5 x 5in, 4 x 37mm, 8 TT
Freccia	DD	It.N	1,220	38	4 x 4.7in, 6 TT
Frondeur	DD	Fra	1,378	33	4 x 5.1in, 2 x 37mm, 6 TT
Fucilere	DD	It.N	1,800	39	5 x 4.7in, 1 x 37mm, 6 TT
Fulmine	DD	It.N	1,238	38	4 x 4.7in, 6 TT
Furious	CV	RN	22,450	29	12 x 4in, 24 x 2pdr, 33 a/c
Furutaka	CA	IJN	9,150	33	6 x 7.9in, 4 x 4.7in, 8 x 24in TT
Fury	DD	RN	1,405	35	4 x 4.7in, 8 TT
G. Garibaldi	CL	It.N	9,400	35	10 x 6in, 8 x 3.9in, 8 x 37mm, 6 TT
Geniere	DD	It.N	1,800	39	5 x 4.7, 1 x 37mm, 6 TT
Georg Thiele	DD	Ger	2,250	38	5 x 5in, 8 TT

Ship	Type	Navy	Tonnage	Kts	Armament
Gioberti	DD	It.N	1,700	39	4 x 4.7in, 2 x 37mm, 6 TT
Glasgow	CL	RN	9,100	32	12 x 6in, 8 x 4in, 6 TT, 2 a/c
Glorious	CV	RN	22,500	29	16 x 4.7in, 24 x 2pdr, 48 a/c
Gloucester	CL	RN	9,400	32	12 x 6in, 8 x 4in, 6 TT, 2 a/c
Gneisenau	CB	Ger	31,800	32	9 x 11in, 12 x 5.9in, 14 x 4.1in, 6TT 4ac
Gorizia	CA	It.N	11,500	32	8 x 8in, 12 x 3.9in, 2 a/c
Graf Spee	Pzs	Ger	12,100	26	6 x 11in, 8 x 5.9in, 6 x 4.1in, 8 TT, 2 a/c
Granatiere	DD	It.N	1,800	39	5 x 4.7, 1 x 37mm, 6 TT
Grecale	DD	It.N	1,640	38	4 x 4.7in, 6 TT
Greyhound	DD	RN	1,350	35	4 x 4.7in, 8 TT
Griffin	DD	RN	1,350	35	4 x 4.7in, 8 TT
Giulio Cesare	BB	It.N	26,140	27	10 x 12.6in, 12 x 4.7in, 8 x 3.9in
Hans Lody	DD	Ger	2,171	38	5 x 5in, 4 x 37mm, 8 TT
Hans Lüdemann	DD	Ger	2,410	38	5 x 5in, 8 TT
Hardy	DD	RN	1,455	36	5 x 4.7in, 8 TT
Hasty	DD	RN	1,340	35	4 x 4.7in, 8 TT
Hatsuyuki	DD	IJN	2,090	34	6 x 5in, 9 x 24in TT
Havock	DD	RN	1,340	35	4 x 4.7in, 8 TT
Hebe	MS	RN	835	17	2 x 4in
Helford	PF	RN	1,370	20	2 x 4in, 10 x 20mm
Hereward	DD	RN	1,340	35	4 x 4.7in, 8 TT
Herman Künne	DD	Ger	2,410	38	5 x 5in, 4 x 37mm, 8 TT
Herman Schoemann	DD	Ger	2,171	38	5 x 5in, 4 x 37mm, 8 TT
Hermione	CL	RN	5,600	33	10 x 5.25in, 8 x 2pdr, 6 TT
Hero	DD	RN	1,340	35	4 x 4.7in, 8 TT
Hobart	CL	RAN	7,100	32	8 x 6in, 8 x 4in, 8 TT, 1 a/c
Hood	CB	RN	42,100	31	8 x 15in, 14 x 4in, 4 TT
Hostile	DD	RN	1,340	35	4 x 4.7in, 8 TT
Hotspur	DD	RN	1,340	35	4 x 4.7in, 8 TT
Hunter	DD	RN	1,340	35	4 x 4.7in, 8 TT
Hurworth	DE	RN	1.050	27	6 x 4in, 4 x 2pdr

Ship	Type	Navy	Tonnage	Kts	Armament
Hyderabad	PF	RN	925	16	1 x 4in, 1 x 2pdr
Hyperion	DD	RN	1,340	35	4 x 4.7in, 8 TT
Icarus	DD	RN	1,370	35	4 x 4.7in, 10 TT
Ilex	DD	RN	1,370	35	4 x 4.7in, 10 TT
Illustrious	CV	RN	23,200	30	16 x 4.5in, 36 – 54 a/c
Iltis	TB	Ger	933	33	3 x 4.1in, 6 TT
Inconstant	DD	RN	1,360	35	4 x 4.7in, 1 x 12pdr, 4 TT
Indomitable	CV	RN	24,680	30	16 x 4.5in, 48 2 pdr, 48 – 54 a/c
Intrepid	DD	RN	1,370	35	4 x 4.7in, 10 TT
Ithuriel	DD	RN	1,360	35	4 x 4.7in, 1 x 12pdr, 4 TT
Jaguar	TB	Ger	933	33	3 x 4.1in, 6 TT
Jamaica	CL	RN	8,525	33	12x 6in, 8 x 4in, 6 TT, 2 a/c
Janus	DD	RN	1,760	36	6 x 4.7in, 4 x 2pdr, 10 TT
Java	CL	Neth	6,670	31	10 x 5.9in, 8 x 40mm, 2 a/c
Javelin	DD	RN	1,760	36	6 x 4.7in, 4 x 2pdr, 10 TT
Jean Bart	BB	Fra	42,800	32	8 x 15in, 9 x 6in, 24 x 3.9in
Jenkins	DD	USN	2,100	37	5 x 5in, 10 TT
Jervis	DD	RN	1,760	36	6 x 4.7in, 4 x 2pdr, 10 TT
Jupiter	DD	RN	1,760	36	6 x 4.7in, 4 x 2pdr, 10 TT
Kandahar	DD	RN	1,760	36	6 x 4.7in, 4 x 2pdr, 10 TT
Karl Galster	DD	Ger	2,410	38	5 x 5in, 8 TT
Kelvin	DD	RN	1,760	36	6 x 4.7in, 4 x 2pdr, 10 TT
Kenya	CL	RN	8,525	33	12x 6in, 8 x 4in, 6 TT, 2 a/c
Keppel	DD	RN	1,480	36	5 x 4.7in, 1 x 3in, 6 TT
Kersaint	DD	Fra	2,441	36	5 x 5.5in, 7 x 21.7in TT
Kimberley	DD	RN	1,760	36	6 x 4.7in, 4 x 2pdr, 10 TT
King George V	BB	RN	35,000	29	10 X 14in, 16 X 5.25in
Kingston	DD	RN	1,760	36	6 x 4.7in, 4 x 2pdr, 10 TT
Kipling	DD	RN	1,760	36	6 x 4.7in, 4 x 2pdr, 10 TT
Kondor	TB	Ger	924	33	3 x 4.1in, 6 TT
Kortenaer	DD	Neth	1,310	36	4 x 4.7in, 2 x 3in, 6 TT
Kujawiak	DE	Pol	1.050	27	6 x 4in, 4 x 2pdr
L'Alcyon	DD	Fra	1,378	33	4 x 5.1in, 2 x 37mm, 6 TT
La Malouine	PF	RN	925	16	1 x 4in, 1 x 2pdr
Laforey	DD	RN	1,920	36	6 x 4.7in, 1 x 4in, 4 x 2pdr, 4 TT
Lance	DD	RN	1,920	36	8 x 4in, 4 x 2pdr, 2 x 20mm, 8 TT

Ship	Type	Navy	Tonnage	Kts	Armament
Lanciere	DD	It.N	1,800	39	5 x 4.7in, 1 x 37mm, 6 TT
Le Terrible	DD	Fra	2,570	37	5 x 5.5in, 9 x 21.7in TT
Leamington	DE	RN	1,090	35	4 x 4in, 1 x 3in, 12 TT
Leander	CL	RNZN	7,200	32	8 x 6in, 8 x 4in, 8 TT, 1 a/c
Libeccio	DD	It.N	1,640	38	4 x 4.7in, 6 TT
Ledbury	DE	RN	1.050	27	6 x 4in, 4 x 2pdr
Legion	DD	RN	1,920	36	8 x 4in, 4 x 2pdr, 2 x 20mm, 8 TT
Legionario	DD	It.N	1,830	39	5 x 4.7in, 6 TT
Lightning	DD	RN	1,920	36	6 x 4.7in, 1 x 4in, 4 x 2pdr, 4 TT
Littorio	BB	It.N	41,375	28	9 x 15in, 12 x 6in, 12 x 3.5in, 3 a/c
Lively	DD	RN	1,920	36	8 x 4in, 4 x 2pdr, 2 x 20mm, 8 TT
Liverpool	CL	RN	9,400	32	12 x 6in, 8 x 4in, 6 TT, 2 a/c
Lotus	PF	RN	925	16	1 x 4in, 1 x 2pdr
London	CA	RN	10,500	32	8 x 8in, 8 x 4in, 16 x 2pdr, 8 TT, 3 a/c
Lookout	DD	RN	1,920	36	6 x 4.7in, 1 x 4in, 4 x 2pdr, 4 TT
Ludlow	DD	USN	1,630	37	5 x 5in, 10 TT
Lützow	Pzs	Ger	11,700	26	6 x 11in, 8 x 5.9in, 6 x 4.1in, 8 TT, 2 a/c
Lynx	DD	Fra	2,125	35	5 x 5.1in, 2 x 75mm, 6 x 21.7in TT
Mackay	DD	RN	1,530	36	5 x 4.7in, 1 x 3in, 6 TT
Maestrale	DD	It.N	1,640	38	4 x 4.7in, 6 TT
Malaya	BB	RN	31,500	24	8 x 15in, 12 x 6in, 8 x 4in, 3 a/c
Manchester	CL	RN	9,400	32	12 x 6in, 8 x 4in, 6 TT, 2 a/c
Maori	DD	RN	1,960	36	8 x 4.7in, 4 x 2pdr, 4 TT
Marne	DD	RN	1,920	36	6 x 4.7in, 1 x 4in, 4 x 2pdr, 4 TT
Massachusetts	BB	USN	35,000	28	9 x 16in, 20 x 5in, 48 x 40mm, 3 a/c
Matchless	DD	RN	1,920	36	6 x 4.7in, 1 x 4in, 4 x 2pdr, 4 TT
Mayrant	DD	USN	1,500	38	4 x 5in, 16 TT
Middleton	DE	RN	1.050	27	6 x 4in, 4 x 2pdr
Milan	DD	Fra	2,441	36	5 x 5.5in, 4 x 37mm, 6 TT
Minneapolis	CA	USN	9,950	33	9 x 8in, 8 x 5in, 4 a/c
Mitragliere	DD	It.N	1,830	39	5 x 4.7in, 6 TT
Mogador	DD	Fra	2,994	39	8 x 5.5in, 10 x 21.7in TT
Mohawk	DD	RN	1,960	36	8 x 4.7in, 4 x 2pdr, 4 TT
Murphy	DD	USN	1,620	37	4 x 5in, 5 TT
Musketeer	DD	RN	1,920	36	6 x 4.7in, 1 x 4in, 4 x 2pdr, 4 TT

Ship	Type	Navy	Tonnage	Kts	Armament
Muzio Attendolo	CL	It.N	7,550	37	8 x 6in, 6 x 3.9in
Napier	DD	RAN	1,770	36	6 x 4.7in, 1 x 4in, 4 TT
Nelson	BB	RN	33,900	23	9 x 16in, 12 x 6in, 6 x 4.7in, 1 a/c
Neptune	CL	RN	7,200	32	8 x 6in, 8 x 4in, 8 TT, 1 a/c
Nestor	DD	RAN	1,770	36	6 x 4.7in, 1 x 4in, 4 TT
Newcastle	CL	RN	9,100	32	12 x 6in, 8 x 4in, 6 TT, 2 a/c
New York	BB	USN	27,000	21	10 x 14in, 16 x 5in, 8 x 3in, 3 a/c
Nigeria	CL	RN	8,525	33	12x 6in, 8 x 4in, 6 TT, 2 a/c
Nizam	DD	RAN	1,770	36	6 x 4.7in, 1 x 4in, 4 TT
Norfolk	CA	RN	9,925	32	8 x 8in, 8 x 4in, 8 TT 1 a/c
Norman	DD	RAN	1,770	36	6 x 4.7in, 1 x 4in, 4 TT
Nubian	DD	RN	1,960	36	8 x 4.7in, 4 x 2pdr, 4 TT
Obdurate	DD	RN	1,540	36	4 x 4in, 4 x 2pdr, 8 TT
Obedient	DD	RN	1,540	36	4 x 4in, 4 x 2pdr, 8 TT
Offa	DD	RN	1,610	36	4 x 4.7in, 4 x 2pdr, 8 TT
Onslow	DD	RN	1,600	36	4 x 4.7in, 4 x 2pdr, 8 TT
Opportune	DD	RN	1,600	36	4 x 4in, 4 x 2pdr, 8 TT
Oriani	DD	It.N	1,700	39	4 x 4.7in, 2 x 37mm, 6 TT
Oribi	DD	RN	1,610	36	4 x 4.7in, 4 x 2pdr, 8 TT
Orion	CL	RN	7,200	32	8 x 6in, 8 x 4in, 8 TT, 1 a/c
Orwell	DD	RN	1,540	36	4 x 4in, 4 x 2pdr, 8 TT
Pakenham	DD	RN	1,550	36	5 x 4in, 4 x 2pdr, 4 TT
Paladin	DD	RN	1,550	36	5 x 4in, 4 x 2pdr, 4 TT
Palomares	AX	RN	1,895grt	16	6 x 4in, 8 x 2pdr
Partridge	DD	RN	1,550	36	5 x 4in, 4 x 2pdr, 4 TT
Pathfinder	DD	RN	1,550	36	5 x 4in, 4 x 2pdr, 4 TT
Paul Jacobi	DD	Ger	2,171	38	5 x 5in, 4 x 37mm, 8 TT
Penelope	CL	RN	5,250	32	6 x 6in, 8 x 4in, 6 TT, 1 a/c
Penn	DD	RN	1,550	36	5 x 4in, 4 x 2pdr, 4 TT
Perth	CL	RAN	7,100	32	8 x 6in, 8 x 4in, 8 TT, 1 a/c
Philadelphia	CA	USN	10,000	32	15 x 6in, 8 x 5in, 4 x 3pdr, 4 a/c
Phoebe	CL	RN	5,600	33	10 x 5.25in, 8 x 2pdr, 6 TT
Poirun	DD	Pol	1,770	36	6 x 4.7in, 1 x 4in, 4 TT
Pola	CA	It.N	11,500	32	8 x 8in, 12 x 3.9in, 2 a/c
Polyanthus	PF	UK	925	16	1 x 4in, 1 x 2pdr

Ship	Type	Navy	Tonnage	Kts	Armament
Poppy	PF	RN	925	16	1 x 4in, 1 x 2pdr
Pozarica	AX	RN	1,895grt	16	6 x 4in, 8 x 2pdr
Primauguet	CL	Fra	7,250	33	8 x 6.1in, 4 x 75mm, 12 TT, 4 a/c
Prince of Wales	BB	RN	35,000	29	10 X 14in, 16 X 5.25in
Prinz Eugen	CA	Ger	14,800	32	8 x 8in, 12 x 4.1in, 12 TT
Provence	BB	Fra	22,190	21	10 13.4in, 14 x 5.5in, 8 x 75mm, 4 a/c
Punjabi	DD	RN	1,960	36	8 X 4.7in, 4 TT
Queen Elizabeth	BB	RN	31,600	24	8 x 15in, 20 x 4.5in, 3 a/c
Quentin	DD	RN	1,705	36	4 x 4.7in, 4 x 2pdr, 8 TT
R. Montecuccoli	CL	It.N	7,550	37	8 x 6in, 6 x 3.9in
Ramillies	BB	RN	29,150	22	8 x 15in, 12 x 6in, 8 x 4in
Ranger	CV	USN	14,500	29	8 x 5in, 86 a/c
Reno	CL	USN	6,000	33	12 x 5in, 16 x 40mm, 6 TT
Renown	CB	RN	32,000	29	6 x 15in, 20 x 4.5in, 8 x 18in TT, 4 a/c
Repulse	CB	RN	32,000	28	6 x 15in, 14 x 4in, 8 x 18in TT, 4 a/c
Resolution	BB	RN	29,150	22	8 x 15in, 12 x 6in, 8 x 4in, 1 a/c
Revenge	BB	RN	29,150	22	8 x 15in, 12 x 6in, 8 x 4in
Rhind	DD	USN	1,500	38	4 x 5in, 16 TT
Rhododendron	PF	RN	925	16	1 x 4in, 1 x 2pdr
Richard Beitzen	DD	Ger	2,232	38	5 x 5in, 4 x 37mm, 8 TT
Rodney	BB	RN	33,900	23	9 x 16in, 12 x 6in, 6 x 4.7in, 2 a/c
Roma	BB	It.N	41,650	28	9 x 15in, 12 x 6in, 12 x 3.5in, 3 a/c
Rowan	DD	USN	1,500	38	4 x 5in, 16 TT
Rye	MS	RN	656	16	1 x 3in, 1 x 2pdr
Saetta	DD	It.N	1,220	38	4 x 4.7in, 6 TT
Sangamon	CVE	USN	11,400	18	2 x 5in, 8 x 40mm, 30 a/c
Santee	CVE	USN	11,400	18	2 x 5in, 8 x 40mm, 30 a/c
Saratoga	CV	USN	33,000	33	20 x 5in, 90 a/c
Saumarez	DD	RN	1,710	36	4 x 4.7in, 8 TT
Savage	DD	RN	1,710	36	4 x 4.5in, 8 TT
Scharnhorst	CB	Ger	31,800	32	9 x 11in, 12 x 5.9in, 14 x 4.1in, 6TT, 2 a/c
Scirocco	DD	It.N	1,640	38	4 x 4.7in, 6 TT
Scorpion	DD	RN	1,710	36	4 x 4.7in, 8 TT
Seeadler	TB	Ger	924	33	3 x 4.1in, 6 TT

Ship	Type	Navy	Tonnage	Kts	Armament
Sheffield	CL	RN	9,100	32	12 x 6in, 8 x 4in, 6 TT, 2 a/c
Shropshire	CA	RAN	9,850	32	8 x 8in, 8 x 4in, 8 TT 1 a/c
Sikh	DD	RN	1,960	36	8 X 4.7in, 4 TT
Simoun	DD	Fra	1,319	33	4 x 5.1in, 2 x 37mm, 6 TT
Sirius	CL	RN	5,600	33	10 x 5.25in, 8 x 2pdr, 6 TT
Somali	DD	RN	1,960	36	8 X 4.7in, 4 TT
Southwold	DE	RN	1,050	27	6 x 4in, 4 x 2pdr
Starling	PR	RN	1,350	20	6 x 4in, 12 x 20mm
Sterett	DD	USN	1,500	37	4 x 5in, 16 TT
Stord	DD	Nor	1,710	36	4 x 4.7in, 8 TT
Strasbourg	BB	Fra	26,500	30	8 x 13in, 16 x 5.1in, 4 a/c
Stuart	DD	RAN	1,530	36	5 x 4.7in, 1 x 3in, 6 TT
Suffolk	CA	RN	10,500	31	8 x 8in, 8 x 4in, 8 x 2pdr, 1 a/c
Suwanee	CVE	USN	11,400	18	2 x 5in, 8 x 40mm, 30 a/c
Swanson	DD	USN	1,630	37	5 x 5in, 10 TT
Sydney	CL	RAN	7,100	32	8 x 6in, 8 x 4in, 8 TT, 1 a/c
T1 – T12	TB	Ger	844	35	1 x4.1in, 6 TT
T13 – T21	TB	Ger	844	35	1 x4.1in, 6 TT
Tartar	DD	RN	1,960	36	8 X 4.7in, 4 TT
Tempête	DD	Fra	1,319	33	4 x 5.1in, 2 x 37mm, 6 TT
Tenedos	DD	RN	905	36	3 x 4in, 4 TT
Tetcott	DE	RN	1,050	27	6 x 4in, 4 x 2pdr
Texas	BB	USN	27,000	21	10 x 14in, 16 x 5in, 8 x 3in, 3 a/c
Theodore Riedel	DD	Ger	2,171	38	5 x 5in, 4 x 37mm, 8 TT
Tigre	DD	Fra	2126	35	5 x 5.1in, 2 x 75mm, 6 x 21.7in TT
Tillman	DD	USN	1,620	37	4 x 5in, 5 TT
Tirpitz	BB	Ger	42,900	29	8 x 15in, 12 x 5.9in, 16 x 4.1in, 6 a/c
Trento	CA	It.N	10,500	35	8 x 8in, 12 x 3.9in, 8 TT, 3 a/c
Trieste	CA	It.N	10,500	35	8 x 8in, 12 x 3.9in, 8 TT, 3 a/c
Tuscaloosa	CA	USN	9,975	33	9 x 8in, 8 x 5in, 2 x 3pdr, 4 a/c
U64	SS	Ger	1,051	18/7	1 x 4.1in, 6 TT
Valiant	BB	RN	31,600	24	8 x 15in, 20 x 4.5in, 3 a/c
Vampire	DD	RAN	1,090	34	4 x 4in, 6 TT
Vansittart	DD	RN	1,090	34	4 x 4.7in, 6 TT
Venus	DD	RN	1,800	36	4 x 4.7in, 8 TT

Ship	Type	Navy	Tonnage	Kts	Armament
Verulam	DD	RN	1,800	36	4 x 4.7in, 8 TT
Vendetta	DD	RAN	1,090	34	4 x 4in, 6 TT
Victorious	CV	RN	23,200	30	16 x 4.5in, 36 – 54 a/c
Vidette	DD	RN	1,090	34	4 x 4in, 6 TT
Vigilant	DD	RN	1,800	36	4 x 4.7in, 8 TT
Virago	DD	RN	1,800	36	4 x 4.7in, 8 TT
Vittorio Veneto	BB	It.N	41,375	28	9 x 15in, 12 x 6in, 12 x 3.5in, 3 a/c
Vivacious	DD	RN	1,090	34	4 x 4in, 1 x 2pdr, 6 TT
Volta	DD	Fra	2,994	39	8 x 5.5in, 10 x 21.7in TT
Vortigern	DD	RN	1,090	34	4 x 4in, 5 TT
Wainwright	DD	USN	1,620	37	5 x 5in, 8 TT
Walpole	DD	RN	1,100	34	4 x 4in, 1 x 2pdr, 6 TT
Warspite	BB	RN	30,600	25	8 X 15in, 8 X 6in, 8 X 4in
Washington	BB	USN	35,000	28	9 x 16in, 20 x 5in, 16 x 1.1in, 3 a/c
Welshman	CM	RN	2,650	40	6 x 4.7in, 160 mines
Westcott	DD	RN	1,090	34	4 x 4in, 6 TT
White Plains	CVE	USN	7,800	19	1 x 5in, 16 x 40mm, 28 a/c
Whitshed	DD	RN	1,120	34	4 x 4.7in, 2 x 2pdr, 6 TT
Wichita	CA	USN	10,000	34	9 x 8in, 8 x 5in, 4 a/c
Wilhelm Heidkamp	D	Ger	2,410	38	5 x 5in, 8 TT
Wilkes	DD	USN	1,630	37	5 x 5in, 10 TT
Wilton	DE	RN	1.050	27	6 x 4in, 4 x 2pdr
Wishart	DD	RN	1,120	35	4 x 4.7in, 6 TT
Witte de With	DD	Neth	1,360	34	4 x 4.7in, 1 x 3in, 6 TT
Wolfgang Zenker	DD	Ger	2,250	38	5 x 5in, 8 TT
Worcester	DD	RN	1,120	34	4 x 4.7in, 2 x 2pdr, 6 TT
Woolsey	DD	USN	1,630	37	5 x 5in, 10 TT
Wrestler	DD	RN	1,090	34	4 x 4in, 6 TT
York	CA	RN	8,250	32	6 x 8in, 4 x 4in, 6 TT, 1 a/c
Z23 – Z34	DD	Ger	2,600	38	5 x 5.9in, 8 TT
Z37 – 39	DD	Ger	2,600	38	5 x 5.9in, 8 TT
Zara	CA	It.N	11,500	32	8 x 8in, 12 x 3.9in, 2 a/c
Zetland	DE	RN	1,050	27	6 x 4in, 4 x 2pdr
Zulu	DD	RN	1,960	36	8 x 4.7in, 4 TT

Selected Bibliography

Battle of the River Plate, Geoffrey Bennett, Ian Allan, 1972.

Chronology of the War at Sea 1939–1945, J. Rohwer & G. Hummelchen, Greenhill Books, revised edition, 1992.

Narvik, Donald Macintyre, Evans Bros. Ltd., 1959.

Navies of the Second World War, a series of informative pocket books covering the British, Dutch, French, German, Japanese, Russian and United States Navies, MacDonald, 1966–1973.

Sea Battles in Close-Up, World War 2, Martin Stephen (edited by Eric Grove), Ian Allan, 1988.

The Battle for the Mediterranean, Donald Macintyre, B.T. Batsford Ltd., 1964.

The Battle of the Atlantic, Jonathan Dimbleby, Penguin Books, 2016.

The Battle of Matapan, S.W.C. Pack, B.T. Batsford Ltd., 1961.

The Battle of Sirte, S.W.C. Pack, Ian Allan, 1975.

The Battles of the Malta Striking Forces, Peter C. Smith & Edwin Walker, Ian Allan, 1974.

The Deadly Stroke, Warren Tute, William Collins Sons & Co. Ltd., 1973.

The Russian Convoys, B.B. Schofield, B.T. Batsford Ltd., 1964.

The Two-Ocean War, Samuel Eliot Morison, Galahad Books, 1997.

The US Navy and the War in Europe, Robert C. Stern, Seaforth Publishing, 2012.

Official publications

Naval Staff History, Battle Summaries (B.R.1736), Nos. 2 (Cape Spada), 5 (Bismarck chase and destruction), 10 (Taranto), 11 (Channel Dash), 24 (Sinking of the Scharnhorst), 26 (River Plate).

Photo Credits

The following abbreviations are used in the image captions to denote the source of each image:

AC   Author's collection
ASM   Air Sea Media Services
BA   Bundesarchiv
NARA   US National Archive and Records Agency
NHIC   US Navy Historic and Information Command
SVL   State Library Victoria (Australia)
WC   via Wikipedia Commons